"In this book Stuart Devenish takes our twenty-first century fascination with the screen and invites us to reenvisage the spiritual life as primarily *visual*, integrating all the spiritual senses into a single lens. Using language that is consistently biblical and Christocentric, Stuart explores the centrality of visual metaphors for the practice of spiritual formation. The Church is called to develop a "catechism of the eye" to enable God's people to adopt a God's-eye point of view. Drawing from his personal journey and the literatures of historic Christianity, Stuart articulates this original reimagining of the task of spiritual theology with freshness and clarity, awakening our stultified imaginations and enlivening our souls. This book is a rich and highly readable resource that shows us how to train the inner eye to be faithful. It is for men and women of faith everywhere who are interested in engaging more deeply in the nurture of souls."

—Robyn Wrigley-Carr
Lecturer and researcher in Christian spirituality,
PhD candidate St. Andrews University, Scotland

"The challenge of disenchantment in the West and the problem of reenchantment have become a particularly significant concern in contemporary spiritual perspective and writing. Many and varied are the responses to this concern, most of which do not bear a specifically Christian character. Stuart Devenish provides us, however, with a remarkable invitation to consider the innate luminosity of the world from a standpoint that is thoroughly and unmistakably Christian. He does so in a language that is both refreshingly engaging and profoundly faithful to the Christian heritage of spiritual wisdom. Christian faith gifts the disciple to see and hear the world in a new way. By exploring this possibility in a way that is informed both from his scholarship and from his own personal journey of learning to see with the eye of faith, Stuart presents us with an entire spiritual framework that underscores and enlivens the responsibility of Christian discipleship. I am confident that as readers enter into and reflect deeply on the insights presented by the author, their own eyes will be touched by the Spirit to see with fresh vision the possibility of being a disciple today."

—Fr. David Ranson
Senior Lecturer in Spirituality,
Catholic Institute of Sydney

"In an age when we are surrounded by new spiritualities of all kinds, Stuart Devenish has wonderfully presented the 2000 year old Christian vision of the spiritual life—as it has been experienced both in the West and the Eastern Orthodox tradition—in a delightfully relevant manner. For this reason this is a very timely book making an important contribution to the biblical vision of our life in Christ beyond denominational strictures. Essentially, the book invites us to begin to read through the lines of material things and to see reality in all of its dimensions as it really is, impregnated and abounding with the very presence of God everywhere. In this sense, "seeing and believing" as the title of the book suggests, becomes the pretext for a comprehensive and nonjudgmental presentation of what St. Paul described a "power to comprehend, with all the saints, what is the breadth and length and height and depth, and to know the love of Christ that surpasses knowledge" (Eph 3:18–19). In reading this work I discovered my own spiritual imagination being both broadened and deepened."

—Dr Philip Kariatlis
Senior Lecturer in Theology,
St. Andrew's Greek Orthodox Theological College

"In our day many visions of the "real" call us hither and yon. In this book Stuart Devenish invites us to learn to gaze again in the direction where Christ would lead us. This book is a persuasive call to renew our commitment to follow Christ, to become attentive to our inner eye, that part of our spiritual lives that alerts us to keener sight. By helping us to see afresh, Stuart calls us to nothing less than a renewing of our faith."

—Dr Michael Frost
Vice Principal Morling Baptist College,
author *Seeing God in the Ordinary*, *Exiles*, and *The Road to Missional*

Seeing and Believing

Seeing and Believing

The Eye of Faith in a Visual Culture

STUART C. DEVENISH

WIPF & STOCK · Eugene, Oregon

SEEING AND BELIEVING
The Eye of Faith in a Visual Culture

Copyright © 2012 Stuart C. Devenish. All rights reserved. Except for brief quotations in critical publications or reviews, no part of this book may be reproduced in any manner without prior written permission from the publisher. Write: Permissions, Wipf and Stock Publishers, 199 W. 8th Ave., Suite 3, Eugene, OR 97401.

Wipf & Stock
An Imprint of Wipf and Stock Publishers
199 W. 8th Ave., Suite 3
Eugene, OR 97401
www.wipfandstock.com

ISBN 13: 978-1-61097-708-1
Manufactured in the U.S.A.

All scripture quotations, unless otherwise indicated, are taken from the Holy Bible, New International Version®, NIV®. Copyright ©1973, 1978, 1984 by Biblica, Inc.™ Used by permission of Zondervan. All rights reserved worldwide.

For my grandson Ethan (b. 2005)
and two of my nieces, sisters Dee and Lyns.
Mind your inner eye.

*The eye is the barometer of the heart;
the warmer the heart the clearer the vision.*

Contents

Foreword xiii
Preface xvii
Acknowledgments xix
Abbreviations and Bible Translations Used xxi
Introduction xxiii
    Focus on the Eye
    Being in Babylon
    Desired Outcomes
    Intended Readers

1 The Eye of Faith 1
    The Age of the Eye
    The Subterranean Life
    Christianity's Invisible Assets
    The Spiritual Senses
    The Eye of Faith
    Conclusion

2 The Eye in Jesus' Ministry 15
    Through Jesus' Eyes
    Jesus' Mission to Eyes and Ears
    The Transfiguration
    The Power of Story
    Seeing through Jesus' Eyes
    Conclusion

x Contents

3 A Visionary Text 26

    A Dangerous Book
    A Visionary Text
    The Scripting Nature of Scripture
    The Third Testament
    Conclusion

4 A Wide-Eyed People 38

    The Interpretive Community
    Participative Knowing
    Christ Plays in Ten Thousand Lives
    Conclusion

5 The Kingdom of Light 51

    The Light of Christ
    Christian Enlightenment
    A Liturgy of Light
    Citizens of Two Worlds
    Conclusion

6 The Way of Wisdom 65

    Mere Christians
    Those Who Are Spiritual
    Christ the Wisdom of God
    The Two Enlightenments
    Conclusion

7 I for Imagination 81

    Enchantment
    The Imaginative Eye
    The Spiritual Imagination
    Some Famous Imaginaries
    Conclusion

8   Toward an Understanding of Christian Spiritual Vision 95
  Contemplative Vision
  Faculties of Faith
  An Eighth-Day Spiritual Theology
  Conclusion

9   Discipling the Eyes 107
  The Age of the Eye Presents Christian Disciples
    with Multiple Distractions
  The Soul is a Seeing Prism Predisposed Variously
    to Soul Sleep and Acute Sight
  The Essence of Faith is Seeing from a Jesus-Eye Point of View
  The Church's Primary Task is to Train the Eye to See Christianly
  Optical Therapy Forms an Essential Part of Spiritual Formation

10   Focusing Your Spiritual Eye 115
  The "Potentials" of the Eye of Faith
  A Postmodern Confession
  Three Prayers

Appendix: On Method 125
Bibliography 129

Foreword

ONE OF THE GREAT historic symbols of the Christian faith is that of "the Word." It has developed into a way of thinking about spiritual things that has been profoundly influential. It is associated with the eternal *logos*, Christ, reason, thought, the Bible, writing, books, preaching and meditation. It has a deep Biblical foundation extending from the constant focus on "the Word of the LORD" in Hebrew thought to the declaration of the apostle John that, "In the beginning was the Word, and the Word was with God." It is the word of life, truth and salvation (Phil 2:16; Eph 1:13, Acts 13:26). A life lived listening to the Word is a life of obedience, discipleship and the proclamation of the word. And the ultimate goal is for the believer to join with the apostle Paul in saying, "I want to know Christ and the power of his resurrection and the fellowship of sharing in his sufferings, becoming like him in his death" (Phil 3:10).

Another profoundly important symbol of faith is that of "vision" which is associated with *seeing* rather than hearing, *light* rather than the word, *illumination* rather than the logos, *images* rather than ideas, *contemplation* rather than meditation and *beauty* rather than reason. It is another way of expressing truth about the spiritual life and it has a Biblical foundation that, as you shall see if you read this fine book, is just as extensive as that of "word." Indeed, the first word of God in Scripture is, "Let there be light!" (Gen 1:3) and one of the final observations in John's Revelation is that in God's new creation there is no need "of the light of a lamp or the light of the sun, for the Lord God will give them light" (Rev 22:5). Seen in this way Christian faith involves a life illumined by the light of Christ and a clarity of vision that enables one to perceive God, oneself, others and the world more deeply than ever before. And the ultimate goal is the vision of God, "Blessed are the pure in heart, for they shall see God" (Matt 5:9).

Sometimes (somewhat ironically) the words of Scripture speak of "seeing" as a way of understanding and believing that is deeper than merely hearing words. At the end of all his reflections Job admits that he had earlier spoken of things he did not understand and he observes, "My ears had heard of you *but now my eyes have seen you* . . . therefore I repent" (Job 42:5). It is seeing that can transform life as the apostle Thomas found so dramatically ("Because you have seen me, you have believed"—John 20:29) and as my good friend Stuart has expounded so well in this book, *Seeing and Believing: the eye of faith in a visual culture*.

Given the book's theme it would perhaps be more appropriate for my words to be placed under the heading "Fore-sight" rather than "Foreword," but however it is expressed, it is a pleasure to commend such an insightful piece of work. Stuart brings to this book a life of ministry and service and his experience of teaching mission, theology and spirituality over a number of years. And in a book dealing with the person in relation to God his expertise in phenomenology as a method for studying religious conversion and spiritual experience is invaluable. He engages in "God-watching," especially as seen in the lives of those close to God, and discusses the inner operations of faith as he works towards four goals: a renewal of Christian *ministry* (can it be seen differently—avoiding the dissatisfactions and inappropriate expectations of ministry that are so common?); a renewal of Christian *discipleship* (so difficult in an age of consumption); a renewal of Christian *spirituality* (in the presence of a multitude of spiritualities) and the reframing of Christian *identity* (one that forms a new vision of reality). This is a book for anyone who yearns to see their relationship with God more clearly. In the Introduction Stuart helpfully describes the intended audience in terms of "saints," "servants" and "seekers" but I would simply say that it is for all those who want to *gaze with intent* upon their relationship with Jesus Christ.

Evelyn Underhill speaks of two kinds of people, "No-Eyes" and "Eyes."[1] The former are those who see only that which can be seen by the physical sense. And so in every area of life they are oblivious to the real significance of whatever they see—the beauty of the world, the reality of suffering and the joy of faith. The "Eyes," however, see differently, they have what we might call an "*in*-sight" that perceives love, goodness, God, faith and hope. And this is because the light by which they see is different. Yesterday I changed the fluorescent light-globe in our walk-in wardrobe and in so doing replaced a "warm-white" with a "day-light" globe. Now our clothes look different. If we learn to see things in the light of Christ then *everything* will appear different. I think I can under-

---

1. Evelyn Underhill, *Practical Mysticism*. New York: E. P. Dutton and Company, ch. 1.

stand the piety of the hymn "Turn your eyes upon Jesus" and the desire to exalt the person of Jesus when it suggests that "the things of earth will grow strangely dim, in the light of his glory and grace" but it is much more the case "that the things of earth become strangely clear in the light of his glory and grace."

This new sight is not found through any mechanical process. It is somewhat mysterious and sometimes dangerous. There is *the mystery of grace* by which Moses sees God. Although Moses is told that he cannot see God for "no-one may see me and live" he is nonetheless described, in the same chapter, as being able to speak with God "face to face, as a man speaks to his friend" (Ex 33). There is *the danger of the illumination* of that which is un-spiritual. Adam and Eve had their eyes opened and they were ashamed of their nakedness (Gen 3:7) and the apostle Paul reminded the Corinthians of the way that God would "bring to light what is hidden in darkness" (1 Cor 4:5). There is also *the need for revelation* because we do not have the power to see what God has not revealed. Initially only John the Baptist was able understand the significance of Jesus ("among you stands one you do not know"—John 1:26). In all of this the experience—and the vision—of the wider Christian community can help us see the way forward. Stuart has brought together ancient wisdom, contemporary culture and his own insights in a way that will help many.

And, finally, all those who are not certain about what they presently see or who wonder whether their vision aligns with the one presented in this book, would do well at least *to begin* to look around at what it contains—perhaps like the fourth figure in Caravaggio's painting of the "Supper at Emmaus." Caravaggio, the brilliant but erratic baroque master painter, depicts the moment at which the two disciples who met the risen Lord Jesus on the road to Emmaus realize who he is. As they share in a meal together and Jesus breaks the bread "their eyes were opened" and the two amazed disciples are shown expressing wonder and amazement. But there is another person present in the picture—a servant or waiter who does not share in the disciples' joy. Yet he leans forward a little and peers at the one the disciples have recognized. Because of their response he is ever so slightly interested . . . What will he do? Will he be able to see what they see? Let us hope that he—and we all—will keep looking because with Christ there is *always* the possibility of "seeing and believing."

Brian Edgar
Professor of Theological Studies,
Asbury Theological Seminary.

Preface

I HAVE SEEN THIS book out of the corner of my eye for what seems like a very long time. When, as a boy, I sat in Aunty Ruth's Sunday school class in my Methodist home church in rural Western Australia, I knew the Bible stories she told us were powerful stories. But somehow I also knew they were not the *only* stories. Later, when I was sent away to boarding school as a pimply-faced teenager and forced to sit through those horrid institutional chapel services, I knew my fellow students and I would have chosen to be somewhere else—if the choice had been ours to make. This is to say, our eyes and ears were attuned to the stories told us by our culture, not the biblical stories we heard in church.

Later, when I encountered Christ for myself as a young adult and became an awe-struck disciple, I knew that the world around me had not changed. But I did know one very powerful thing—that *I* had changed. The biblical stories I had been drinking in had caused me to change my view of the world—profoundly. Thirty-five years have gone by since those dramatic days, and only now have I found the words, the time, and the confidence to explore what has become, for me, a near lifelong attempt to understand the spiritual dimension unfolding within me. But I have noticed a second powerful thing—that even as I have struggled to bring clarity and focus to my own personal spiritual life, the Christian church in the Western world has been undergoing an epic struggle of its own. Its struggle has been to retain its unique vision of the world, a vision shaped by the biblical stories, in what has become a *visual* culture. A synchronicity exists between my personal journey toward self-understanding and the current crisis of the Western church. This is what has fascinated me and prompted me to write as I have. My approach is to bring together the spiritual eye that operates in Christian discipleship with the predominating visuality of contemporary culture to "see what happened"—not unlike a science experiment. I will leave the reader to determine whether I have been successful in my spiritual experiment.

Acknowledgments

I WANT TO ACKNOWLEDGE a great many people who have supported me as I have wrestled with my life, my faith, my ministry, and my scholarship. Without their help, guidance, and wisdom I doubt this book would ever have seen the light of day. To name just a few of the people who have contributed to my life and faith journey: my father Robert Devenish (d. 1997), who understood these things but was not able to say them; Liz and Trevor Sykes, who have been mentors and friends for over thirty years; John Olley, my seminary President who taught me how to think; Wilfried Otterbach, my senior missionary in Manila who convinced me to buy my first computer; Ian Hawley, who provoked me to think more deeply about conversion and the spiritual life; Trish Sherwood, my PhD supervisor who showed me there was more to see when one looked phenomenologically; Alan Gordon, who has never stopped encouraging me; Neville and Joan Cooper, saints whose lives inspired me; Alan Hirsch, a missional innovator and fellow traveler; Keith and Val Butler, true friends and (in Val's case) my spiritual director; Ros Gooden, whose hunger to know and understand has always impressed me; the NationsHeart Church of Christ in Canberra, whose congregation showed me what the kingdom of God looked like; the Modbury Church of Christ in Adelaide, whose congregation patiently listened to me talk out parts of the initial draft of this manuscript; Mark Woloszyn, who invited me to think more deeply about the teachings of Eastern Orthodox Christianity; and my wonderful wife Ros, who always believed I had something to say to the world. Thank you to each of you.

I particularly want to thank my colleagues in the Australasian Centre for Studies in Spirituality, Martin Dowson, Maureen Miner, and Marie-Thérèse Proctor, with whom I have shared a journey of discovery into the meaning of spiritual experience and the inner world of the religious believer since 2007. Their friendship and support have been invaluable, and their expertise in psychology and the psychospiritual dimensions found in the human person have been most instructive.

I want to acknowledge the encouragement and support of my fellow editors for the Crucible e-journal (http://www.ea.org.au/crucible/welcome.htm): Brian Edgar, Glen O'Brien, Ian Packer, and Darren Cronshaw. Their desire to provoke fresh thinking about the Christian faith, making it both intelligible and accessible, is outstanding.

I wish also to express my appreciation to the many people who have read the various drafts and iterations of this book, many more than are named here. Those whose feedback and comments have left their mark on the work in some way are Liz and Trevor Sykes, Maureen Miner, Martin Dowson, Liz Hentschel, Alan Gordon, Chris Dall, Trevor Riley, Rick and Heather Lewis, Glen O'Brien, and Martin Robinson.

Special thanks to Bruce Haddon who read several chapters of the book in its early draft form and gave assiduous feedback. Bruce has also contributed two pieces of creative writing that add an extra dimension to the overall work. I am deeply grateful to Bruce for his creativity and generosity.

I owe particular thanks to Anna McHugh for helping me find my "voice" as a writer. Her wise editorial advice directed toward the revision of several early chapters is highly valued. Also, I am deeply grateful to Fr. David Ranson (Roman Catholic) and Philip Kariatlis (Greek Orthodox) for reading the manuscript in its final stages. Their guidance regarding the spiritual understandings and practices that operate within their respective traditions within the larger Christian community is much appreciated. Thank you.

Finally, my thanks to the faculty, staff, and students at The Salvation Army Booth College in Sydney where I have taught for the past three years. Their hospitality, collegiality, and engagement with the spiritual life have been an inspiration to me.

While I owe my thanks to each of these people in different ways and have benefited greatly from their input, any mistakes, oversights, or errors of judgment that remain in this text are mine alone. I acknowledge there is always more to learn, know, experience, and understand.

Stuart Devenish, Melbourne, Easter, 2012

Abbreviations and Bible Translations Used

KJV—King James Version

NASV—New American Standard Version

NIV—New International Version

NRSV—New Revised Standard Version

RSV—Revised Standard Version

The Message—Eugene Peterson's translation of the Bible

Introduction

It is no surprise that human beings find other human beings hugely fascinating. A favorite pastime for many of us is to sit in a public thoroughfare with a cup of coffee in our hands and watch the world go by. People hurry past this way and that, to where and for what only they know. Each person has his or her own story to tell and destiny to fulfil. Everyone draws upon a vision of life located in some deep place within. Some are free to follow the light inside, while others are barely aware that light exists to alleviate their darkness. Why do we find other people so fascinating? Is it perhaps because we find glimpses of our own selves in the faces of others?

It is also no surprise that human beings find God and the idea of the supernatural immensely fascinating. History, geography, and culture are filled with great artifacts that describe humanity's interactions with the sacred. Human beings have created great temples and places of worship that reflect the glory of the divine. These places are rife with wondrous artwork, and replete with great stories of human response to the celestial invitation. God—it can be said—is one of the human family's truly magnificent obsessions. In our own time, religion and the possibility of God have somehow become separated in the Western psyche. This has caused a season of anxiety about the place of God and our interactions with the sacred. Despite a new visibility of religion in the media, politics, and society, we are far from experiencing a full-scale return to a time when "God is in his heaven and all is well on earth." In other words, we are in the process of renegotiating the possibility of God and the place of religion. For the moment, let me simply say that this book is intended to make a contribution to that renegotiation.

This book is a study in people watching, but people watching from a particular point of view. For over twenty years I have had an enduring interest in the human person in the divine presence. In particular, I have been interested in the kinds of modifications to thinking and acting that arise when a person is exposed to ideas that originate from "the other side." This is to say, I am interested in people who have God on their minds. My aim in this book is to undertake an extended study of the interior life of the Christian believer by looking through the lens of the eye of faith. In so doing, I am endeavoring to come to an understanding of what the true believer sees, knows, and believes about themselves, God, and life itself. To facilitate this inquiry, I will situate the reader at the center of the believing soul who identifies himself or herself as a Christian disciple.[2] The key words for this exploration are spirituality, believing soul, discipleship, insight, luminescence, transformation, and optical "therapy."

Thanks to the tremendous scientific advances we have made in the twentieth and early twenty-first centuries, we have a profound understanding about the human body and the world we live in. Likewise, spirituality is receiving a great deal of attention from many quarters. But we do not yet have a modern way of adequately understanding what spirituality is: we do not have a shared language for describing its component parts or how it functions in the human person. One of the goals of this book is to make a contribution to that understanding, with particular reference to the lived experience of the Christian believer.

This book is also a study in God-watching. Even though God cannot be directly observed (as theologians sometimes seem to assume), and we cannot see God as he is in himself, we can observe him in the lives of those people who identify themselves as belonging to him. We can perceive him by understanding the order of creation, by reading the words of the Bible, and by observing the lives of those who make their confession, "I believe." Although "no one may see [God] and live" (Exod 33:20), important traces of God's character and attitude to the world can be observed in the lives of the faithful. As we will discover, seeing God is not something carnal, fleshly eyes are capable of. The capacity to see God is something which is given to human creatures as a result of God's decision to show himself to humanity. "The fruit of submission is revelation."[3] Likewise, understanding how belief influences the confessing community's outlook on the world requires a deep,

---

2. The phrase "believing soul" comes from Paul Ricoeur, *Symbolism of Evil*, 19.

3. An insightful phrase used by Terry Walling of Leader Breakthru, (http://www.leaderbreakthru.com/), in a real-time seminar on leadership transitions in Sydney, September 2011. With permission.

spiritually-informed awareness. Such things are not immediately given, but require a profound attentiveness to the spiritual dynamics at work in the enlivened human person's mode of perception.

It is not possible to identify a God's-eye perspective completely, because human beings do not have the capacity for such great knowledge. We are, after all, far from being all-knowing, all-seeing, and all-glorious creatures. It is not possible for a finite human person to hold the entire substance of God and reality in mind. To lay claim to such knowledge is nonsense. But spiritually speaking, a God's-eye point of view—however imperfectly formed—can be observed in the convictions of Jesus' disciples here on earth. This is the consistent testimony of confessing faithful communities across the two thousand year-long history of Christian spirituality. If we are going to come to understand the inner lives of disciples, we must first come to grips with the invisible realities they claim to see. In effect, if we are to understand their words and actions in the physical dimension, we need to try to see what they have seen in the spiritual dimension. And if we are going to undertake the processes that lead to the spiritual formation of saints, we need to understand how their spiritual senses are activated, operated, and developed towards Christ-likeness and maturity. This is where the optics of faith comes into focus for us: as readers of the life stories of the saints, as observers of the Christian faith, and as practitioners of Christian spirituality ourselves. In a visual culture, understanding how the eye of faith functions and its role as the primary mode of perception in the lives of the saints is non-negotiable. The saint's platform for viewing God becomes our platform for viewing saints.

FOCUS ON THE EYE

Jesus spoke of the eye as the "lamp of the body" (Matt 6:22), and many people since have spoken of the eyes as the "gateway to the soul." I suggest three things can be learned about the spiritual life by focusing on the eye of faith. First, looking into the eye of faith enables us to observe a great deal about the inner operations of faith inside the believing soul (i.e., how the believer thinks and what it is they see and know). Medical doctors routinely measure blood pressure in order to assess their patient's general state of physical health. Measuring blood pressure allows health professionals to "read" the signs of health or disease in the human body. Because the spiritual life is interior to a person and is not immediately observable, it is reasonable for spiritual guides to find equivalent points of entry into an individual's spiritual life to assess the vital signs of the soul. Looking in through the eye of faith allows spiritual guides to understand the inner functioning of the soul and to diagnose its health and diseases. Spiritually speaking, the eye is the barometer of the heart; the warmer the heart the clearer the vision. This makes the spiritual eye an exceptionally translucent measure of the life of the soul.

Second, the eye of faith provides a unique access point into the inner life of the believing soul. It enables us to observe how an individual interprets and comprehends reality. Looking in through the eye allows us to "read" the mind of the believer and to discern the manner and extent to which he or she uses the Jesus-story to interpret his or her life in order to reconstitute it into a sacred life. And third, looking in through the eye enables us to identify the level of illumination in an individual's soul and to gauge a disciple's willingness to go further on the spiritual journey, deeper towards self-discovery, and on into the life of God.

By focusing on the eye of faith we, as outside observers, are able to see that the true believer looks through the appearances of the outward world to distinguish the spiritual reality that lies within and beyond it. As a result of the real things a believer has seen, he or she makes the confession, "I believe." Even when no God can be seen with the naked eye, and even when a counter vision of the real is rejected by opinion makers in the culture, believers still insist on claiming that what they have seen is trustworthy and real. In fact, so compelling is the vision seen through the eye of faith that believers make costly choices to live in poverty, to forego sex and worldly pleasure, to serve others rather than their own interests, and to spend their lives in service of the "cause" of the kingdom of God—for the sake of Christ. So the eye of faith is not something useless and impractical. It is something real and of great importance to the church in the crisis of the present moment. As strange as it might seem, the eye of faith is one of the central features of the Christian spiritual life.

The questions that will guide our inquiry are: What is this vision that has grasped the imaginations of close to one third of the world's population today, not to mention the faithful throughout history? How does this faith vision function, what is its significance, and what is its relevance for the growing spiritual interest we see in the West at the present time?

BEING IN BABYLON

When the apostle Peter wrote his pastoral epistle to the persecuted Christians in Asia Minor towards the end of the first century AD, he concluded it with greetings from "She who is in Babylon" (1 Pet 5:13). It is a strange greeting because Peter actually wrote from Rome, not Babylon. Commentators agree that this greeting is a cryptic reference to Rome's brutal and repressive rule over its inhabitants. By the first century, Rome was the center of political and military supremacy across the known world. To the early Christians it represented a godless and intimidating presence. To enable him to make sense of the circumstances, Peter reached back in time to recall Israel's earlier exile to Babylon—the capital city of the much-feared Babylonians—to warn believers in his day of the dangers they faced. Christians had experienced a season of persecution, causing them to question God's ability to overcome his enemies. In those uncertain times Peter sought to strengthen the faith of the wavering saints by reassuring them of the certainty of God's victory and the coming glory of his kingdom. The imminent return of the "Day of the Lord" and God's power to overcome his enemies rang a note of eschatological certainty. There in Rome, in the face of the dragon, so to speak, the apostle Peter recognized the need to maintain his own faith vision of the "coming of the Lord" and his imminent thousand-year-long reign. And Peter made the strengthening of the spiritual eyesight of his tremulous audience the centerpiece of his pastoral strategy. We learn the lesson from the early church that maintaining Christ as the center of its faith vision for an extended season is difficult, and this is especially true in times of persecution and intimidation.

Peter's words have direct application to today's Christians who live in a world that sometimes feels like Babylon. In our world today, the claims Christians make about the Lordship of Christ and the reality of the kingdom of God are easily challenged by other visions—both secular and religious—about what is real. Whereas at one time Christianity informed the imagination and worldview of almost the whole of Western society, now the church is a shadow of its former self, and its once-powerful voice has become a faint whisper. Ours is a post-Christian era. It is *post*-Christian because this era is the season that comes after Christianity. It is post-*Christian* because the once widely acknowledged benefits of the Christian faith are now treated with suspicion and sometimes even with contempt by the dominant, non-Christian culture. Yet, at the same time, a strange counterdevelopment is also unfolding. In addition to this being a post-Christian era, the current widespread interest in spirituality marks this out as a post-secular era. It is *post*-secular because it comes after the era when secularism reigned in our culture. And it is post-*secular* because many religions and forms of spirituality have sprung up in place of the Christian faith. People appear to need and want the refreshing resources offered by spirituality to enliven and energize their inner lives, but they do not want big-R religion making demands on them. For saints, being Christian in a post-Christian and a post-secular society poses unique challenges (on the one hand) and presents unique opportunities (on the other).

It is helpful for contemporary Christians to "reach back"—as the apostle Peter did—to earlier times in order to remember God's faithfulness to his anguished people. In our "time between times" there is need to hold onto the great Christian hope of Christ at work in the world, hidden from full view yet whispering his gospel in mercy before he returns in power to rescue his people and to the thunder his judgment on his enemies. Holding onto and maintaining spiritual vision is one of the most important things Christian communities can do in today's world. It is a season of waiting—even anxious waiting. But as we wait, we are developing an exilic consciousness whose central attribute is a clarified and heightened vision of the coming of the great day of the Lord. And we continue to pray "Your kingdom come," even if there are (as yet) few observable signs of its presence.

DESIRED OUTCOMES

These are interesting times for the Christian faith and Christian believers; times that need to be carefully discerned. My wrestling with the important themes of the eye of faith and spiritual vision in what is without doubt a predominantly visual culture, arose directly out of what I have seen in the churches in the lives of saints wherever I have traveled. I have observed a deep disquiet in the minds of many Christians. I wish to argue that these themes demand exploration, on the grounds that they have a direct bearing on the lived experience of saints in the twenty-first century, and may hold the key to the future wellbeing of Christianity in the Western world. To that extent I argue that they require careful attention, as well as deep insight and understanding. I am a fellow traveler, "caught up" in the wrestle to make sense of our times. I invite you to come on a journey of discovery with me; a journey that is not only of academic interest but also of personal, communal, and even global significance. Let the reader understand.

I have four aims for this book.

THE RENEWAL OF CHRISTIAN MINISTRY

Ministry leaders (or, servants, as I refer to them in this book) are responsible for providing spiritual nurture to the men and women, boys and girls under their care. In keeping with Jesus' charge to Peter to "feed my sheep" (John 21:17), ministry leaders have an apostolic mandate to exercise the "cure of souls" as over-shepherds of God's people, for whom they must give account. Yet the default model of ministry inherited by most ministerial leaders from previous generations is more managerial than spiritual. While their calling is to the ministry of prayer and the preaching and teaching of the Word, many ministry leaders find themselves waiting on tables in actual practice. Clearly, they did not sign up to become leaders of (religious) corporations, accountants of the church's financial ledger, or caretakers of the church roster. Most pastors I know want more than anything else to fulfill a Moses-type function for their congregations, standing between God and their people in order to convey the truth of Christ, the blessing of God, and the life of the Spirit. They do not want to be religious waiters—but that is what many have become.

Christian ministry as it is practiced today by most pastoral leaders is very different from what they signed up for. They have learned how to count, organize, and manage saints, but few have the training, expertise, or awareness to identify the real spiritual needs of the souls they encounter in their congregations week by week. As over-shepherds, many somehow lack the confidence and a clear understanding of how to shepherd people toward genuine spiritual growth that will enable them to cultivate the mind of Christ, the faith of an apostle, the heart of a prophet, and the convictions of a saint. Constant wrestling with their own spiritual needs and dealing with conflict in their churches leads to high rates of burnout, job dissatisfaction, and psychological stress in ministry leaders. But leading people deeper into the presence of Christ and teaching them how to use the glass of vision that forms the centerpiece of the Christian spiritual life, is a deeply satisfying and highly stimulating activity. It is what ministry servants signed up for and long to do. It has the potential to provide high levels of job satisfaction for ministry leaders and to launch saints under their care on a deeply satisfying faith experience that is unshakeable.

THE RENEWAL OF CHRISTIAN DISCIPLESHIP

We live in an "undisciplined" age. Gabriel and Lang have described the conspicuous consumption that defines Western society as unmanageable and unsustainable.[4] A new order of values underpins today's society, a society that is not based on preservation and savings but on spending reinforced by a state-sponsored doctrine that prioritizes politics and the economy over peoples' moral and spiritual development. Like their unbelieving neighbors, Christians grow up under the tutelage of the media that teaches them to believe what is good for General Motors is good for America. In the meantime we find it difficult to remember Jesus' teaching that "man does not live on bread alone, but by every word that proceeds from the mouth of God" (Matt 4:4). Maintaining a focus on the kingdom of God and living a faith-based life is often difficult when—as the poet William Wordsworth averred—"the world is too much with us," and when we are not trained to maintain our spiritual vision in the face of the many counter visions thrust upon us by the changing values of society. One of the central roles of church leaders in times of transition is the presentation of the Christian vision through teaching and modeling, to maintain and build up the faith of those who believe. It is critical that church leaders know how to operate the eye of faith in their own spiritual lives, and are able to teach those under their care to focus their eyes on Christ and to dilate their eye of faith wide open. It is critical they guide believers between the dual dimensions of the material world in which they live their everyday lives and the spiritual world that is the cornerstone of their belief system and identity. Here is where church leaders discover the central importance of the eye of faith for the practice of the Christian spiritual life in the world.

---

4. Gabriel and Lang, *Unmanageable Consumer*, 8–9.

Becoming a saint is not simply becoming morally virtuous—although that is one noteworthy characteristic of discipleship. Becoming a saint means to learn to look through the lens of the eye of faith and to see things from a God's-eye point-of-view. Discipleship is vision, and disciples are visionaries. The renewal of Christian discipleship in a world blinded by material things and an image-soaked, media-driven culture is—I suggest—dependant on learning to refocus the eye of faith, both as a ministry priority and a central factor in the practice of Christian spirituality. Like going to the optician to be fitted with a new prescription for reading glasses, becoming a saint requires that we learn how to see things from Christ's point of view. Learning to "read" our lives using the palette of root metaphors provided by the biblical narratives is central to learning to look, think and behave like a disciple of Christ. A root metaphor is an image or fact that shapes as individual's—and indeed the entire church's—perception of reality. The root metaphors provided in the Bible all draw their reference points from the sin-salvation-sanctification hermeneutic that forms the center of the unfolding narrative of the Christian story.

THE RENEWAL OF CHRISTIAN SPIRITUALITY

Spirituality is currently experiencing newfound interest throughout our inner cities, suburbs, and regional communities. It is not "Christian" spirituality that is piquing the interest of would-be practitioners, but every shade of older religious forms such as Kabbalah, Tibetan Buddhism, and Wicca; and the newer forms of spirituality focused on the god within, Reiki healing practices, and tantric sex. A tidal convergence is occurring where two things are happening at once: first, ours is a post-secular age where the numinous and the transcendent (especially the idea of self-transcendence) are achieving new levels of popularity; but second, public opinion is turning against Christianity leading to our era becoming a post-Christian era. Many people have come to view Christianity as distasteful and even offensive. Tragically, the genius of Christian spirituality is being lost in these tidal flows. Potentially we have millions of primed spiritual seekers in our communities, few of whom have any idea of the treasures that exist in Christian spirituality or have any inclination to undertake their spiritual journeys in the context of the Christian spiritual tradition.

Why is this? I think the fault lies not so much with responsive seekers outside the church but with a loss of spiritual confidence inside the church, which in turn has affected Christians' ability to stand their ground and maintain their testimony in the face of multiple challenges that besiege them in the twenty-first century.

How do we begin to overcome this problem? We can start by studying the concerns of those saints who precede us. In the golden period of early monasticism, what monks—especially the desert hermits—feared most was acedia. Acedia is a loss of spiritual alertness and attentiveness that leads to a dissipation of spiritual desire. Monks who suffered from this spiritual affliction were warned to "Wake up!" and were then returned to their prayers with a renewed vigilance. Acedia can be understood as the greatest spiritual failing of Christendom. But thanks to an alert monasticism, these early Christians were awake to the threat acedia represented. But in the post-Christian era, the greatest spiritual fault likely to beset saints is myopia. Myopia is the slow incremental loss of spiritual vision. The physical defect of macular degeneration erodes first the peripheral and then the central vision of the sufferer, resulting in a loss of color and clarity of objects in the viewer's line of sight. Similarly, the spiritual defect of myopia causes a loss of spiritual sight and results in a growing sense of detachment between the believer and Christ. In the face of the challenges represented by the encroaching religions and spiritualities, secularism and consumerism, it is vital that Christians who want to sustain a vibrant spiritual life pay attention to recovering and maintaining their spiritual sight. Overcoming the besetting sin of myopia requires us to sharpen our vision. The only prescription capable of producing a reawakened and restored Christian faith is a renewed encounter with Christ that produces the euphoric confession, "We have seen the Lord" (John 20:25).

THE REFRAMING OF CHRISTIAN IDENTITY

We have already noted the loss of spiritual identity experienced by many Christian believers. That identity has been depleted by the values of Western liberal democracy whose secularizing, liberalizing, and pluralizing forces have worked to undermine the faith of many in the church, and have called the cornerstone beliefs of Christianity into question.

Maintaining the vision at the center of Christian belief in an unbelieving world is enormously difficult—but it is also enormously important. Holding on to one's identity as a follower of Christ is not easy when the faith one professes is no longer in government, but has been relegated to the status of opposition. If we are to find our way forward, we need to take stock of where we are in the present flow of history, intentionally move to renew our vision in order to see God's hand in the midst of the chaos, and consciously reframe our identity as followers of Christ.

Markers of religious identity vary. Jewish believers share a common ethnicity, a universal language, a communal performance of the prescribed food laws, and a common commitment to male circumcision. Muslim believers share a common language, a universal confession, a common prayer ritual, and an expectation of pilgrimage to Mecca. Those external signs are unmistakable markers of religious identity in those two faiths. However, Christian religious identity imposes no such uniformity of ethnicity, language, worship style, or expression. This is perhaps one of the great strengths of the Christian faith. The front door is wide open—"whosoever will may come."[5] While Jesus required his followers to observe two basic ritual acts in baptism and participation in the Eucharist or communion, he imposed no requirement on his followers other than to love him. The most notable markers of Christian identity are not external but internal.

Central to a disciple's follower-ship after Jesus is his or her confession that Jesus is the Son of God and the Savior of the world. Each disciple is to offer him their singular allegiance. And disciples are to take his earthly life as the template on which to model their own lives, and embrace his teaching regarding the kingdom of God and use it as their guide. The quality of life expressed in a disciple's community is to parallel the qualities of the kingdom Jesus taught about in the Sermon on the Mount (Matt 5–7). And disciples are to adopt an understanding that interprets the world through the lens of a supernatural, Christ-centered and redemptive hermeneutic that gives shape to the Christian self-awareness. While an academic perspective might describe Christian behavior "from the outside" as communal, confessional, or sacramental, a spiritual perspective that looks at Christian identity "from the inside"

---

5. A phrase often heard in churches with reference to the openness of the scope of salvation. It originates from Revelation 22:17, KJV.

will identify Christian behavior in terms of the luminous vision of reality that characterizes the supernatural-existential perspective peculiar to the confessing saint.[6] It is from the transformed center of a changed life inside the believing soul that they are able to project their new vision of reality outward onto the canvas of the everyday world through their actions and demeanor. "The disruption of divine love, the 'resurrection experience,' the 'call to conversion' experienced as grace, reconfigures the coordinates by which all of life is interpreted."[7]

INTENDED READERS

This book is intended for an educated lay readership among a predominantly Christian audience. In particular, it is addressed to three groups of readers I will call *saints*, *servants*, and *seekers*.

Saints are worshipping Christians who live an active and vital faith life, and who make up the worship services, Bible studies, prayer meetings, and outreach groups of local congregations. While they may not always be perfect, they know themselves to be called to perfection. The times in which we live are confusing times for the church, and I have observed that many Christians in local churches are demoralized. A focus on the eye of faith will enable believers to better understand themselves and the faith that functions in them as being "the faith once and for all delivered to the saints" (Jude 3).

At this point a word of explanation needs to be made for Roman Catholic and Eastern Orthodox readers. My use of the word *saints* returns to the biblical use of the word. In this use, saints are not canonized individuals admitted to the bench of the ecclesial elite. Rather, saints refers to *all* those who have been made holy or righteous by their faith in Christ. In other words, from a biblical point of view, anyone who places Christ at the center of their lives can properly be called a saint. I use the term *saints* in this way because ours is a critical moment in the life of the Christian faith in the Western world. The renewal of the Christian vision and the capacity for Christian saints to look, see, perceive, and act Christianly is of first-order importance. Removing logs from our own

---

6. Rahner, "Supernatural Existential," in Reno, 117, 124.
7. Hall, "Choosing Life or Second Life?" 19.

eyes and increasing our capacity to see through Jesus' eyes is the urgent need of the moment.

Servants are ministry leaders who "serve" in the churches. Whether they be ordained clergy in the form of pastors and priests or lay leaders with responsibility for the pastoral oversight and spiritual formation of those under their care, they have been charged by Christ to "Feed my sheep" (John 21:17). Such feeding is intended to grow sinners into saints, sheep into shepherds, and beginners into seasoned believers. This is a functional maturity. Disciples are required to reproduce Jesus' life in their own lives. To be a disciple is effectively to "copy a life." With regard to their own lives, servants are to fulfil their calling as human beings remade in the image of Christ. With regard to God, their lives are to add to his glory and renown. And with regard to the wider world, the quality of their lives and testimonies are to do two things. First, it is to generate numbers of like-minded disciples who—along with them—also desire to make Christ the first priority in their lives. And second, it is to produce a better world modeled on the kingdom of God, which originated in Jesus' life and teaching.

Shepherds in today's churches need to be released from the current fascination for management, leadership, and pushing souls around. A new preference needs to be adopted that favors the growing of existing saints and the making of new ones. If there are no healthy, growing saints, no effective mission can occur. If there is no mission, there will be no new Christians. Adopting a focus on the eye of faith will enable ministry leaders to move back to the pastoral cutting edge by refocusing their ministries on teaching, spiritual formation, and a renewed commitment to the normative expectation of producing growth in the spiritual life. That means servants must keep the spiritual welfare of their congregations firmly in their sights, and work on ways to lead people under their care toward spiritual maturity as a matter of first priority. In effect, a focus on the eye of faith elevates the role and function of ministerial leaders to that of spiritual leaders, specialists in the inner life, and respected guides for the journey.

Seekers, or spiritual beginners, are often left on the margins. But because of their energy, commitment, and the radical response they frequently make to Christ, they have much to contribute; but they also have much to learn. The church as a whole owes seekers an explanation of what a uniquely Christian spirituality is and how it functions in their lives. This explanation is especially needed when there are multiple spiritual options available to a seeker. Seekers are right to ask questions about which pathways are valid and why the Christian "way" is more trustworthy than others. After all, seekers presently going through their conversion experiences, or who have just emerged from them, want to know how the spiritual life works! They are hungry for teaching that explains the radical transformation they have just experienced. Explaining these truths in simple language to beginners actually helps those of us who are further advanced in the faith. It allows saints and servants alike to recover a proper perspective on the faith they may have held for many years, and it also demands that teachers remain spiritually fresh; otherwise, they have nothing to offer their younger fellow travellers. To become citizens of the kingdom of God, even while remaining citizens of this world, requires beginners and seasoned travelers alike to understand the inner dynamics of faith at work within them. An exploration of spiritual sight as a faculty of faith is a recognizable and transferable way of communicating the substance of the Christian faith to spiritual seekers.

These introductory thoughts have prepared us to turn our attention to the first chapter of this book, which addresses the important topic of the spiritual eye.

1

The Eye of Faith

*"The eye is the lamp of your body; when your eye is clear,
your whole body also is full of light"* (Luke 11:34 NAS).

IN THIS FIRST CHAPTER, we will examine the topic of the eye of faith and the role it plays in the life of the Christian believer. We will explore the concept of spiritual vision and the central role it plays in the Christian spiritual life. My aim in this first chapter is to invite you to think about the importance of the eye of faith in your spiritual life, and to open your eyes to the greater possibilities that arise when we bring the concepts of believing and seeing together.

THE AGE OF THE EYE

The twenty-first century is the age of the eye. All versions of technology, including televisions, computer screens, the Internet, and so on, have become our points of contact with other people and indeed the world. We are immersed in visuality. We spend our days working in front of computers with our faces lit by the fake light of electronic displays. We spend our evenings sitting in front of yet more screens, entertaining ourselves in order to reclaim our sanity. No wonder Guy Dubord has suggested we live in a "society of spectacle," whose cornerstones are the news media, simulated events, and electronic performances.[1] The twenty-first century is visual to its core. The media reaches into our lives through the eye of the camera, and we reach out to the world through the medium of the electronic screen. Reality has become image centered

---

1. Dubord, in Blocker, *Seeing Witness*, 13.

for residents of our media-saturated society. We are living in the *age of the eye*. I want to put forward an argument that links the visuality of contemporary postmodern society with the visuality that occurs in the inner life of the soul. There is a remarkable correlation between the way we live our lives in the media-soaked postmodern world and the way the soul functions through perception and spiritual sight. In the society of spectacle, to which Dubord draws our attention, we have come to rely on the visual and the virtual in our everyday lives. Seeing and sensing are at the forefront of the way we humans engage with our surroundings. The media—represented by television, theater, cinema, and most strikingly the Internet—are uniquely designed to facilitate humanity's need to reach beyond ourselves to become fully present to circumstances in the physical and social spaces around us. As we participate in this visual and perceptual activity, we experience a certain level of intimacy with the high drama of global politics, the financial variations of the stock markets, the marvellous achievements of sporting athletes, and the triumphs and tragedies of socialites and movie stars. This is "our" world, and we want to know what's going on. But there is also a certain distance between us and these people and events, caused mostly by the fact that we have no preexisting relationship with them, and the digital technology seems (at first) to get in the way of any meaningful relational contact. However, once we get comfortable with the digitally enhanced interface, we no longer feel that the technological intermediary blocks our relationship but actually facilitates it. Think of the first time you ever wore 3-D glasses. At first it felt strange, but soon it came to feel natural and comfortable. Obviously, people can overcome the sense of distance, and cross the boundaries technology presents, and move towards intimacy. A glance at the many dating websites available on the Internet shows this to be true.

The spiritual life is to a large extent a visual life. The overwhelming desire of the worshipping soul is to contemplate the face of God and to experience the river of delights found in his presence. But finding one's way into and navigating one's way around the spiritual realm is not easy. It demands that we exercise a form of spiritual perception and insight that takes effort and requires attention. Like seeing in the dark, we are dependent on finding a light source capable of illumining our path, or waiting until our eyes adjust to the deep twilight, in order to distinguish the shadowy shapes in front of us. When it comes to the spiritual life, there is no digital interface to help us navigate our way through the spiritual realm. Instead, we have something even better. We have the Spirit of God indwelling our lives to enliven our understanding and awareness. The importance and role of the Holy Spirit cannot be underestimated in the spiritual life. The Spirit alerts, awakens, reminds, teaches, reveals, and enlightens us to the things of God. Yet there is also a human role in this process of becoming aware and making our spiritual eyes open and clear so that our whole body can be filled with light (Luke 11:34). Christian disciples have an obligation to pay attention to their mode of spiritual seeing so their eyesight is not "nearsighted" (2 Pet 1:9) but capable of "see[ing] heaven opened" (Acts 7:56).

I want to suggest the idea that visuality is so central to the spiritual life that it parallels and exceeds the visuality that is central to our digitally enhanced postmodern existence. Christian spirituality depends on the eye of faith to orient itself in spirit spaces and to enable us to take our Godward journey into places that are, at first, unknown to us. Over time and with growing familiarity, we come to know and understand the spiritual realities we encounter in the life of faith. Our journey with God—or godfaring—is dependent on us coming to see, know, and participate in spiritual realities that cannot be seen by the physical eye but must be apprehended by the eye of faith.[2] Upon first use, operating the eye of faith feels strange (think of those 3-D glasses); but once we have adjusted to this way of seeing the strangeness fades and the sense of intimacy and wonder becomes all-encompassing. This is our life, and we don't want anything to block our pathway into the new life Christ offers us.

> O world invisible we view thee;
> O world intangible we touch thee;
> O world unknowable we know thee;
> Inapprehensible we clutch thee.[3]

The concept of the eye of faith provides a congenial point of connection between the Christian spiritual life *and* contemporary postmodern culture. There is a remarkable coherence between the way social media is modeled on, and augments, the physical eye—enlarging our engagement with the world and extending our consciousness—and the way the

---

2 Clark, *Godfaring*, 2000.
3. Thomson, "In No Strange Land," 247.

mysterious inner operations of the soul depend on the eye of faith to inform and illumine its path forward on its journey into the life of God. Although the visual interface provided by the Internet is digital and technological, the interface that properly belongs to the spiritual life is a normal function of the soul's capacity to grasp the infinite and the eternal. To this extent the digital revolution in which we are participants—as impressive as it is—can only ever be an incomplete facsimile of the internal operations of the soul. The spiritual life is a seeing life. So we ask the questions: What does Christianity have to offer the age of the eye and what would make the society of spectacle want to peer into Christian spirituality's treasure trove to find answers to its deepest questions and resources that meet its deepest needs? For those whose eyes are opened to spiritual reality and alert to the growing sense of hunger that contemporary society expresses for what will satisfy its deep-seated longings, the present moment is one of profound opportunity and possibility.

THE SUBTERRANEAN LIFE

The Christian disciple lives in the gap between heaven and earth. Whereas our earthly life is open to observation, the impassioned spiritual life that boils within us remains hidden and mysterious. To that extent our spiritual lives are subterranean, hidden from view under a blanket of fog. Luci Shaw compares this state of in-between-ness to an amphibious life.[4] In just the same way that frogs are able to live in the dual environments of land and water—and in fact need both to survive—so the Christian believer lives in and needs the physical world and the spiritual world. We are called to "work out our salvation" in the earthly sphere with fear and trembling (Phil 3:12), while at the same time "fix[ing] our eyes on Jesus" (Heb 12:2) in the heavenly realm. In order to live simultaneously in these two overlapping and intersecting worlds, we need to learn how to operate the eye of faith, which enables us to identify and observe Christ's presence in every aspect of our daily lives. "Learning to be amphibious, that is, adapting to life in two radically divergent realms, the heavenly and the earthly, demands of us that we learn to see again, through different lenses than those to which we have become accustomed."[5] If we

---

4. Shaw, "Living in the Gap," 172–3.
5. Ibid., 171.

are to truly worship Jesus, we must first know him; and in order to know him, we must first have the capacity to perceive his presence in our lives and our world. As with the early disciples, followership after Jesus is highly dependent on being with him and "observing" his character and actions in order to learn from him. To this extent, knowing how to locate Jesus' presence in our lives and our worlds is a first-order priority for the Christian saint.

Heaven—or the spiritual dimension that exists there—is a world without boundary or limit. We can surmise that it is deeply transparent. From our reading of the Scriptures we are able to say it is characterized by an unclouded lucidity.[6] Everything in the spiritual realm can be seen, known, and understood for what it is in its purest translucent essence. *Truth is reality unveiled.* While God is hidden to the residents of this world because he dwells "in unapproachable light" (1 Tim 6:16), in the spiritual dimension God is fully known to both his subjects and his enemies alike. We are told that the angels who are charged with the care of human beings "always look on the face of my Father who is in heaven" (Matt 18:10). There, in that dimension, everything that can be known about God is made completely manifest—totally seeable. That is why the four living creatures in the eternal present constantly offer worship and the twenty-four elders cast their crowns before the throne exclaiming, "You are worthy, our Lord and God, to receive glory and honor and power" (Rev 4:9–11). Those who dwell in heaven can worship God truly because they see him truly. And that is why it is said "the demons believe—and shudder!" (Jas 2:19). And those who are graciously granted entry to heaven can expect to see the Almighty "face to face" on the last day.

But this world is a different matter altogether. Our physical world is characterised by murkiness and multiple obstructions. Although God's presence is embedded in every corner of creation, his nature is spelled out to us in riddles and hieroglyphs. If we remain a mystery to ourselves, what hope do we have of understanding God through the mute medium of nature? Of course, poets and natural theologians such as Gerard Manley Hopkins, Annie Dillard, and Thomas Merton point out that the natural world is a theater on whose stage God reveals himself

---

6. For example see Luke 16:23, where the rich man in the parable of the rich man and Lazarus sees Abraham far away in heaven, and entreats him to send Lazarus to slake his thirst.

and enacts his purposes. Those whose souls are awakened have a habit of seeing this. Hopkins is right to tell us that the "world is charged with the grandeur of God."[7] As a metaphysical artist, God's best work is done in nature's fabric. Emonet has written, "To know God, one must begin by regarding the things God has made, and what God has given them of perfection in the roots of their very being."[8] Nature and this earthly life are never to be mistaken for enemies or strangers by the godfaring pilgrim, but as the stage on which the drama is set or the workshop where their offering is prepared. While redemption was conceived and commanded in heaven, it must be played out here on earth. During our mortal lives, the only address that redemption has is here on earth! That is why all the metaphors of the spiritual life—including the new birth, the table in the wilderness, and light in dark places—are earthly images that serve to amplify and enlarge the sacred themes of salvation. In fact, these metaphors for redemption employ the language and imagery of everyday life in order to emphasise that even those who have lived the humblest and most mortal lives are welcome in glory. Yet from where we presently stand, we "see as in a glass darkly" (1 Cor 13:12 KJV). The knowledge of heaven is not given to us immediately, but must be constantly sought out. As Luci Shaw suggests, we have a "now-you-see-him, now-you-don't" God who scatters signs and clues of his identity around creation and the human mind like a paper trial, so that he often appears tantalisingly near—but seems strangely distant at the same time.[9] The whole point of pilgrimage is to continue resolute on the quest, and to weather the rigors of mental and spiritual (and often physical) exhaustion that beset us by staying awake and alert to the reality of God, even if our physical senses seem grossly inept for the task.

When it comes to the spiritual world, we all start out on our journeys blind and mute. Samuel Shoemaker discussed how people search for the door into the kingdom of God in his poem, "I Stand at the Door."[10]

> They creep along the wall like a blind man,
> With outstretched, groping hands,
> Feeling for a door, knowing there must be a door,
> Yet they never find it.

7. Hopkins, "God's Grandeur," 27.
8. Emonet, *God Seen in the Mirror*, 44.
9. Shaw, "Living in the Gap," 180.
10. Shoemaker, "I Stand at the Door," 53.

> ... Men die outside the door, as starving beggars die
> On cold nights in cruel cities in the dead of winter.
> Die for want of what is within their grasp.
> They live on the other side of it—live because
>   they have not found it.

Not knowing what we dumbly detect in front of us is humbling. If only there were some way to make the invisible visible! In his wonderful children's adventure *The Voyage of the Dawn Treader*, C. S. Lewis described a scene in which Lucy was sent into the sorcerer's castle by the dufflepud Chief Voice to open the magician's book and locate the spell that makes "hidden things visible."[11] In just the same way that we do not have a technology of the soul to call upon (as we do in the digital world), neither do we have a spell to make the furniture of the spiritual realm appear to us. Yet our blindness is not permanent. Through prayer and deep discernment, blindness gives way to the magnificent vision of faith that is the central feature of Christian spiritual experience. There are many pathways into the walled garden that is the spiritual life. We simply have to learn how to open our eyes—with the help and guidance of the Spirit—to find the gate that gives us entry.

CHRISTIANITY'S INVISIBLE ASSETS

In investment banking it is common practice to list a company's assets under different headings. Most commonly they fall under headings such as cash and plant, stocks and bonds, hired staff and intellectual property, or something similar. But often those assets are further divided into visible and invisible assets. Visible assets are physical objects such as buildings, warehoused stock, and manufacturing machinery that can be listed on a company's books for auditors to examine. Whereas invisible assets are items of a more intangible nature, such as anticipated future profits, brand recognition, and market share. These items cannot be easily placed on a company's asset register, even if they characterize an organization's creative genius or prestigious heritage. These invisible assets nonetheless form part of the equity upon which the company trades and justifies further investment in its future.

---

11. Lewis, *Voyage of the Dawn Treader*, 341.

We do not often think of our spiritual lives in terms of visible and invisible assets, but it can be a helpful device. There are two ways we usually encounter religion: the outward and the inward. Over its collective two-thousand-year-long history, Christian communities have accrued a vast treasury of assets. Examples of Christianity's outward visible assets are its cathedrals and churches, schools and colleges, hospitals and charitable houses, monasteries and mission agencies. All these arose from people's earnest inward responses to Jesus' invitation to "Come, follow me" (Matt 4:19). These visible assets can be measured and valued, sold or exchanged, and will pass away when their fabric succumbs to time.

Christianity's invisible assets cannot be seen by the naked eye but are more valuable than visible assets because they neither devalue nor disintegrate with the passing of time. Unlike a cathedral that can be seen with the visible eye, the invisible assets of faith can only be seen by the eye of faith. Invisible faith is the wellspring—the reason why people build visible artifacts of faith in the first place. An inventory of Christianity's invisible assets would be the envy of any broker: certain knowledge of the existence and nature of God, Jesus' humanity and divinity, the kingdom of God, salvation, eternal life, righteousness, the great Christian hope, the second coming of Christ, and the promised new heaven and new earth. These invisible realities exert a powerful influence on the thought-lives of believers. They exist as real presences in the lives of worshippers who participate in Christianity's two-thousand-year-long spiritual tradition that commenced with the earliest apostles. These invisible realities give shape and substance to the believer's earthly life, causing them to reevaluate their physical existence through the prism of that greater world. Like the earth's magnetic north, the reality upon which Christian experience bases itself is a real but invisible force. Its power is not diminished even though it is unseen in the everyday world. Rather, those who confess faith in Christ understand the physical world on the basis of the transformative logic provided by heaven and strive to apprehend its realities in ever-clearer terms. Indeed, they insist that the teachings of the Christian faith contained in the creeds and doctrines all unswervingly point to those unchanging spiritual certainties on which the physical world is based and upon which its provenance rests.

THE SPIRITUAL SENSES

Under ordinary circumstances, the senses of taste, touch, smell, sight, and hearing are given to us at birth. We must learn to use these gifts through trial and error, constant use, and fine-tuning. Each of the senses is perfectly matched to the physical objects they were intended to connect with. This is basic to our human existence. The taste of chocolate, the texture of silk, the smell of coffee, the sound of jazz, and the sight of beauty all are experiences each of us knows and understands well. As adults we engage in the sensuous activities of life in an unconscious and undifferentiated way. Once we have learned how to manage these organic bodily senses, we engage with the world without having to think about how we do it—we just do it.

There are also spiritual senses available to us. But because these are less well-recognized and used less frequently, we have to think harder about how we use them and the kinds of things we focus them on. Often they are also less well-developed, requiring us to pay more careful attention to how we use them. Out of the many different schools of wisdom found in Christian history, one thinks of writers who have contributed to our understanding of the spiritual senses, such as St. Augustine (354–430), Gregory of Nyssa (330–395), Richard of St. Victor (d. 1173), Bonaventure (1221–1274), William of Auxerre (1150–1231), Thomas Aquinas (1224–1274), Hildegard of Bingen (1098–1179), Julian of Norwich (1342–1413), Teresa of Avila (1515–1582), St. John of the Cross (1542–1591), and Teresa of Lisieux (1873–1897). Each of these individuals in their different, but important, ways have suggested that exercising and operating the *sensus fidei* (the faith senses) plays a central role in the spiritual life.[12] These spiritual writers remain important to Christians of every generation as they are trustworthy guides for those explorers who undertake the journey inward.

So, how can we transcend the limits of our infirm senses to come to "see" Christ for ourselves? The believing soul deeply desires contact with the spiritual world. The spiritual senses enable us to observe the spiritual world and to "draw near" (Jas 4:8 RSV) to Christ. The spiritual senses parallel the way the physical senses of seeing, touching, tasting, smelling, and hearing function, but there are important differences. Spiritual senses are not located in the somatic matrix of our bodies. Rather, they

---

12. Rush, *Eyes of Faith*, 66.

describe the way the soul functions in a quest to apprehend spiritual realities. In his first epistle, John, the beloved disciple, suggests that hearing, seeing, and touching are central to the act of bearing testimony to Jesus (1 John 1:2–3). Origen (ca. 185–ca. 254) suggested there are five spiritual senses, each of which enables the believer to use the senses of sight, hearing, taste, touch, and smell in order to experience the delights of God.[13]

Hildegard of Bingen referred to the spiritual senses as "visual thinking" that integrate both reason and experience.[14] Meister Eckhart (1260–1327) is well-known for his statement, "The eye with which I see God is exactly the same eye with which God sees me. My eye and God's eye are one eye, one seeing, one knowledge, and one love."[15] Eckhart seems to suggest the eye is a form of two-way spiritual diaphragm that enables God to know and see us, but which also enables us to see and know God. But our limited vision of God does not limit God's unfettered vision of us. A text from the *Philokalia* affirms that God watches his subjects, and the writers take pains to encourage their readers to "Make every effort to call God to mind, for He is looking at you, and whatever you are thinking in your heart is plainly visible to him."[16]

Eastern Orthodox Christianity pays special attention to spiritual vision as a primary aspect of the spiritual life. Like the apostle Paul's elevation into the third heaven where he saw things that did not rightfully belong to mortal creatures, the Eastern tradition believes that making a commitment to contemplative prayer and the holy life can enable us to participate in a vision of spiritual truth that returns us to our creational innocence. Instead of delaying the possibility of seeing God until some post-death beatific vision, Orthodoxy argues that the future glories of the saints in heaven can be brought forward into the present moment for those who believe in the here and now. This does not mean that the spiritual life is one long ecstatic moment. Rather, it is often a difficult road that sometimes leaves us feeling we are alone and in the dark. What it does mean is that the spiritual life invites us to enter into

---

13. Origen's third Homily on Leviticus, in Coolman, *Knowing God*, 28.
14. Caviness, "Artist: To See, Hear, and Know," 111.
15. Eckhart, *Sermon 16*, 179.
16. Palmer et al., *Philokalia*, 28. The Philokalia is a collection of texts written between the fourth and the fifteenth centuries by spiritual masters of the Orthodox Christian tradition.

a lifelong conversation with God that requires sustained and deliberate attention. It requires that we fix our eyes attentively on Jesus; hence, the prayer commonly prayed by Orthodox believers: "Lord, enlighten my darkness!"

THE EYE OF FAITH

If we are committed to living the spiritual life, we may often feel there is a noticeable discrepancy between the effectiveness of our everyday eyesight (if we have good eyes, that is) and the ineffectiveness of our spiritual vision. The whole point of living the spiritual life is to grasp the spiritual reality we cannot see with our physical eyes, but which makes itself known to our spiritual senses as something really real. If we are to grasp these unseen realities, we must become adept at seeing and perceiving the unseen sacred realm—even as we continue to live our lives as physical creatures. This is the challenge that confronts anyone aspiring to live the spiritual life and who sets their sail to catch the wind of the Spirit. Looking, seeking, orienting, perceiving—are all routine activities of the soul. "Where has your lover gone, most beautiful of women? Which way did your lover turn, that we may look for him with you?" (Song 6:1).

Seeing is believing, so the saying goes. Trained as they are in the art of rational scepticism learned through our Western scientific education, our minds find it hard to give up the certainty of rational proof in favor of subjective evidence. But in our everyday lives we often reach for things that do not meet the criteria of proof in order to find resources for our everyday lives. There are lots of things that cannot be seen by the naked eye, but which are essential for our existence. These form the substance of our lives. Just a sample of such real but unseen things are memory, love, emotion, character, happiness, wonder, awe, beauty, hope, anticipation, and our highest ideals. These are the foundations on which we build our lives and which bring us our brightest joys. Yet they remain hidden from view inside our inner beings, while at the same time they supply the set of defining principles from which we weave the fabric of our lives as material persons.

But beyond the seeing-is-believing option there exists a second, more real, possibility of believing-is-seeing: or what we call faith. There are many people who assert that faith is blind, but that is to misunderstand faith. Faith is not blind; it is an acute form of sight. The writer to the Hebrews defined faith as "being sure of what we hope for and certain of what we do not see" (Heb 11:1). In other words, the eye of faith, trained in the art of spiritual seeing and thoroughly informed in its knowledge of the Christian life, through what it has learned by reading the Scriptures, has the capacity to make invisible things visible through the eye of faith. The defining characteristic of those faith-filled people mentioned in Hebrews, chapter 11, is that they all practiced the art of spiritual seeing, and they set their compass by what they "saw." They were required to "fix [their] eyes on Jesus, the author and perfector of [their] faith" (Heb 12:2). Even Jesus himself exercised the same counterpoint form of vision (although in a much greater way) as he "turned his face toward Jerusalem" (Luke 9:51 RSV) to go to the cross. Jesus embraced a future glory that had been revealed to him by the Father, before it was ever a historical fact. It required the eye of faith to see it. Jesus was committed to using the eye of faith in his earthly life. And as we shall see in the next chapter, the bulk of his ministry was directed toward training the disciples in how to use the eye of faith.

The average person is spiritually asleep, and the usual state of human awareness is dull. For most of us, our spiritual eyes are closed to anything except our immediate desires and physical appetites. But it is the nature of the spiritual life to be awakened! "Awake O sleeper, rise from the dead, and Christ will shine on you" (Eph 5:14). In order to be awakened we must first be converted. Jesus spoke of the need for the "new birth" (John 3:7), which is the most fundamental transformation of the Christian faith. Only the reborn person, who has the life of the Spirit of God within, is truly awake to the spiritual realities that surround him or her. This is where the eye of faith comes in. Believing contains within itself the capacity for seeing. Jesus himself provided us with the meaning of testimony when he said, "We speak of what we know, and we testify to what we have seen" (John 3:11). Christianity is more a matter of perception than of proof. Sight is a central feature of the spiritual life. But we must be clear about what we mean by sight.

What do we mean by spiritual sight? Spiritual sight is not actual sight but applies the metaphor of the inner eye to explore how we can employ the figure of physical sight to spiritual discernment. When we "see" into the spiritual dimension to discern God at work in our lives, we do not actually see him with our physical eyes. Rather, we discern his invisible presence at work in the visible world by "reading" circumstances in such a way that we attribute events and circumstances to the purposeful actions of a loving God rather than to the meaningless unfolding of random events. Spiritual sight is like insight. Insight is related to wisdom and a heightened capacity for spiritual perception, discernment, and knowledge in Christian discipleship. Such insights can be described as an awakening to the truth of something through a penetrating mental vision that enables the viewer to grasp the inward meaning of an event or circumstance. The viewer applies the hermeneutic of the supernatural-redemptive-restorative hermeneutic learned in the reading of the Scriptures to their life circumstances. "To become a Christian involves learning the story of Israel and of Jesus well enough to interpret and experience oneself and one's world in its terms."[17] Knowing the biblical drama—which von Balthasar calls a *theo-drama*—enables the spiritual viewer to know which meaning to apply to what event or circumstance.[18] As a result of undergoing the transformation of the new birth, of reading the Bible, adopting its supernatural horizons, and adjusting their lives to the sin-salvation-sanctification drama they find there, believers have a new point of reference from which to interpret the world. Insight represents a form of awakened and inspired wisdom. For the Christian, the object of faith is always the person of Jesus Christ; and the off-shoot of faith is insight, which is the peculiar possession of all those who believe.

As Isaac of Nineveh (d. 700) wrote, "Faith is the doorway to the mysteries. What the eyes of the body are for physical objects, faith is for the hidden eyes of the soul."[19] The Eastern Orthodox tradition emphasizes that the eye is the primary organ of faith, thus giving primacy to spiritual sight as the most compelling characteristic of the human person in the divine presence. Like the living creatures in Ezekiel's vision, the soul is understood to become "all eye." "As the [Orthodox understanding of] icons suggests, the whole person becomes vision, filled with a light that issues from the face of the transfigured Christ."[20] By now you will have come to understand that the eye of faith is an integrating theme that ties the spiritual senses together into a single lens to enable Christian believ-

---

17. Lindbeck, *Nature of Doctrine*, 34.
18. von Balthasar, *Theo-Drama*, 1983.
19. Clement, *Roots of Christian Mysticism*, 213.
20. Ibid., 248.

ers to take into their souls the sacrament of truth, and then project that divine spectacle of truth outward onto the canvas of the world.

CONCLUSION

We began this chapter with Jesus' teaching on the importance of the eye for the Christian disciple: "The eye is the lamp of your body; when your eye is clear, your whole body also is full of light; but when it is bad, your body also is full of darkness" (Luke 11:34 NAS). Human beings are visual creatures. But often our knowledge of the spiritual realm is impoverished to such an extent that we are effectively blind to its existence. We often see things out of the corner of our eye, but we do not know what it is we are seeing. In our blindness we find it difficult to respond to God's invitation to participate in the divine life. Becoming a Christian means being aware of the inadequacy of seeing through the physical eye and learning how—with the Spirit's help—to see through the spiritual eye. Becoming a Christian means exchanging visions; turning away from the one-dimensional vision of a self-centered and self-directed life in order to embrace a new multi-dimensional life that has Christ at its center. "Through 'seeing' him one becomes a disciple."[21] This insight is consistent with the church's two-thousand-year-long conviction that faith is deeply visional.

When we come to faith we come to see things, know things, and understand things that do not belong to us natively. Following conversion and the change that occurs in the heart, Christian disciples become "seers" of the supernatural, "hearers" of mysteries, "tasters" of divinity, and "touchers" of the mountain of God. This book is an operator's manual for the Christian soul, using the spiritual eye as its point of reference. It aims to name those spiritual dynamics that operate within the believing soul in order to contribute to an increased understanding on the part of the saint, of the dynamics of the life of the Spirit within each one. "The soul is at the divine center; it is a part of us that sees and knows God. There can be no integrity without the voice of the soul, no true sense of vocation without the soul's direction, and no fruitful discernment without the soul's-eye-view."[22]

---

21. Kerkhofs, *Horizon of Kindly Light*, 51.
22. Kelcourse, "Finding Faith," 61.

2

The Eye in Jesus' Ministry

"Blessed are your eyes because they see" (Matt 13:16).

THIS SECOND CHAPTER EXPLORES Jesus' use of the eye in his ministry. Jesus had much to say about eyes—more than we might previously have imagined. The chapter begins by looking into Jesus' eyes, and ends by suggesting that Jesus looks into his followers' eyes to ensure that they have learned to see themselves and the world from his Jesus'-eye point of view. My aim in this chapter is to invite you to consider the extent to which you see yourself and the world from a Jesus'-eye point of view.

THROUGH JESUS' EYES

Have you ever wondered what Jesus looked like? Was he so ordinary looking that he deserved no second look (as Isaiah seems to imply in Isaiah 53:2) or was he strikingly handsome (as artists in every age are obliged to portray their subjects)? One thing is certain, "Whoever Jesus was or was not . . . he was a man once, whatever else he may have been. And he had a man's face, a human face."[1] The history of Christian art shows that we appropriate Jesus into our own worlds, making him to fit our particular ethnic and cultural profile. If we are white, we imagine Jesus as being like us. If we are brown, we imagine Jesus as being like us. If we are black, we imagine Jesus as being like us. There is nothing wrong with this inclination because Jesus lived his life and gave it up for all people everywhere. There is a certain universality about Jesus. He is the man for all seasons and for all peoples. Though for reasons of

---

1. Buechner, *Face of Jesus*, vii.

historical accuracy, we ought to acknowledge that he himself wore the russet-brown skin of the Middle Eastern Jewish race. It is amazing that the biblical writers did not concern themselves with what Jesus looked like. To our knowledge, no attempts were made by the earliest eyewitnesses to depict his face. "The writers of the New Testament give no description of [Jesus' face] because it was his life alive inside them that was the news they hawked rather than the color of his eyes."[2] Yet for all that, Jesus' eyes retain a great deal of significance. Their significance lies not so much in their color, or even what he saw through them. What is of critical importance is *how* he looked; that is, the interpreting mode he applied to everything he saw through his eyes. It is this particular feature that causes us to claim that Jesus' eyes are of the utmost importance. In effect, we are trying to look through Jesus' eyes to discover how he saw things.

The key to understanding Jesus is to understand his self-conception. How he understood himself is paradigmatic to understanding his whole identity and mission. And how he understood himself is rooted in his relationship with his Father and the implications that relationship had for his role as the one who was to inaugurate the kingdom of God. Out of his own convincing encounters with his Father, Jesus gained the perspective he needed to apply a radically new form of interpretation to his life as a human person with a face. He came to understand that his face was indeed "the face of God."

There are three possible scenarios when it comes to understanding Jesus' self-identity. The first scenario is that Jesus understood himself to be a good Jew who strove to fulfill the requirements of the law by obeying the teachings of the patriarchs and prophets. In this scenario, any inner rumblings that may have caused him to suspect he had a special relationship with God were treated with suspicion by both himself and anyone with whom he may have confided his leanings. Second Temple Judaism allowed, even encouraged, different expressions of worship to make room for the needs of the far-flung Jewish diaspora to worship in the languages and cultural forms of their host communities. But it did not look kindly on theological dissent. In this scenario Jesus would have been reined in and reincorporated back into the bosom of Judaism. This first scenario resulted from a false reading of what God intended, and resulted in a false understanding of Jesus' identity.

2. Ibid., ix.

The second possible scenario is that Jesus understood himself to be a prophet in the long line of Jewish prophets like Moses, Elijah, and Jeremiah. These individuals understood themselves to have been appointed by Yahweh as his designated agents in the unfolding drama of salvation. Under the conditions of this scenario, Jesus' annunciation of the coming kingdom was no more than an extension of the ancient prophecies concerning the *ebed Yahweh* ("the servant of God") whose faithful obedience was a precondition for the outworking of the purposes of God in the world. As Yahweh's prophet, Jesus' task would have been to restore the tradition by calling the people to return to the central teachings of the Jewish faith around the themes of covenantal living (fulfilling the obligations of the Ten Commandments), obedience to God (including refraining from the worship of idols and false gods), and living justly with their Jewish and non-Jewish neighbors (Israel's mission to the nations). This second scenario (falsely) assumed that Jesus' role in God's purposes was only that of a bit player, not the main actor who was to become the centerpiece of God's plan of salvation history.

But, as the third possible scenario will show, the first two scenarios do not take proper account of the full extent of Jesus' experience of God. A sequence of events occurred in Jesus' life which, when put together, formed an incontrovertible impression in his mind that he was more than a good Jew and more than a Jewish prophet. First, there was the wealth of Old Testament prophecies relating to the coming of the Messiah. For example, "The Lord your God will raise up for you a prophet like me from among your own brothers. You must listen to him" (Deut 18:15) and "But you, Bethlehem Ephrathah, though you are small among the clans of Judah, out of you will come for me one who will rule over Israel, whose origins are from old, from ancient times" (Mic 5:2). Second, there were the birth narratives that were filled with miraculous events and preparatory signs. Because "Mary treasured up all these things and pondered them in her heart" (Luke 2:19), she would have passed these on to Jesus with his mother's milk. These markers would have given the young Jesus much pause for thought as he prepared for and reflected on his ministry. And third, alongside the habit of prayer set in his adult life, which provided him with ample opportunity to hear from God, Jesus experienced a series of significant events, such as his baptism and his transfiguration where God's voice thundered from heaven, "This is my Son, whom I love; with him I am well pleased" (Matt 3:17). From these events and a lingering memory of his preexistent relationship with the Father, Jesus grew to have what has come to be called a "filial consciousness." He understood himself to be God's appointed messiah who fulfilled the Old Testament categories of prophet, priest, and king; and because of this he was willing to accept titles such as the "son of David," "son of man," "Lord," and "Master" during his lifetime. It was on the basis of this radical self-consciousness that Jesus was able to identify himself as "One greater than the temple" (Matt 12:61); and to make such statements as, "before Abraham was, I *Am*" (John 8:58); and "I and the Father are one" (John 10:30). Jesus applied a revisionist interpretation that reframed the whole of salvation history around himself as its center, with the kingdom of God as the extent of his righteous rule and reign. Jesus was not a bit player but the lead actor in the unfolding drama of God's redemptive history.

JESUS' MISSION TO EYES AND EARS

Jesus took his job description seriously. He took it from the passage in Luke 4:18–19: "The Spirit of the Lord is on me, to preach good news to the poor. He has sent me to proclaim freedom for the prisoners and recovery of sight to the blind, to release the oppressed, to proclaim the year of the Lord's favor." That text has its origins in the Old Testament narrative of Isaiah 61:1–2, where the people of Israel had lost their spiritual edge and were doing civic religion, formal religion, easy religion. They were invited to "walk in the light of the Lord" (2:5), but they continued to "[exchange] darkness for light and light for darkness" (5:20), mistakenly assuming that they were "wise in their own eyes" (5:21). The young prophet Isaiah was commissioned to declare to his forgetful and backslidden audience: "Be ever hearing, but never understanding; be ever seeing, but never perceiving. Make the heart of this people calloused; make their ears dull and close their eyes. Otherwise they might see with their eyes, hear with their ears, understand with their hearts, and turn and be healed" (Isa 6:9–10).

Isaiah's task was not to harden the hearts of his fellow Israelites, because they were already hardened. His mission was to announce judgment as an act of loving correction on God's part and to invite recalcitrant Israel to rediscover the pathways of grace and return home from their exilic wanderings. Jesus' ministry picked up where Isaiah's ministry left off, focusing not on pronouncing judgment but on inviting his first-century audience to pay attention to their mode of seeing and hearing what God was doing and saying to them. Whereas Jesus' first-century audience was comprised of the people of Israel, the Jewish religious leaders, and their gentile neighbors; his subsequent audience today is vastly more diversified than his first-century hearers. The faith that originated with Jesus' teachings has now become a truly global faith. But the central issue remains the same regardless of the time or place of his listeners. Jesus' call to us is to see differently; in fact, *to see as he saw.*

Jesus' mission was to open the eyes and ears of his audience. Some have suggested that Jesus' healing of the blind man at Bethsaida (Mark 8:22–26) is a metaphor for the awakening to insight regarding Jesus' identity. The first phase of the two-stage healing process allowed the blind man to see, but only "like trees walking around." Living by the religious teachings of the Pharisees led their followers into darkness and confusion. But in the second phase of the two-stage healing a second application of spittle produced clear vision in the man. The healing of the blind man is a parable intended as a rebuke to the religious authorities, in that right spiritual teaching and insight does not come from the Pharisees who were "blind guides" (Matt 15:14) but from Jesus who gives the gift of sight. Jesus invited his audience to attend to his teaching, which reflected a more pristine version of God's perspective. If it can be said that to God alone "belongs wisdom and power; counsel and understanding are his" (Job 12:13); Jesus has now become the son in whom all of God's wisdom and knowledge can be found in concentrated form. "The work of God is this: to believe in the one he has sent" (John 6:29). Jesus invited his audience to "think again" (the meaning of the Greek word for repentance, *metanoia*, is based on *meta*, "another" and *nous*, "mind"). His never-ending probing: "Do you not yet believe?" and the impatient "How much longer must I be with you!" indicates Jesus' appeal for people to understand his teaching and to adopt the same unique interpretation of the Jewish Scriptures, history, and identity that he himself had come to adopt.

The eye is a central feature of Jesus' teaching throughout the Gospels; and once alerted to this fact, everywhere the reader looks the eyes feature prominently in his teaching.

- (Matt 6:23) The *eye* is the lamp of the body. If your eyes are good, your whole body will be full of light. But if your eyes are bad, your whole body will be full of darkness. If then the light within you is darkness, how great is that darkness!
- (Matt 13:16–17) But blessed are your *eyes* because they see, and your ears because they hear. For I tell you the truth, many prophets and righteous men longed to see what you see but did not see it, and to hear what you hear but did not hear it.
- (John 7:24) Stop judging by *mere appearances*, and make a right judgment.

Jesus came to inaugurate the kingdom of God through his life, teachings, miracles, and, ultimately, through his death, resurrection, and ascension. Although the unseen kingdom was manifest in the quality of his exceptional life, nevertheless his disciples and followers were required to exercise the eye of faith in order to perceive the reality of the presence of the kingdom. The Lord's Prayer (Matt 6:9–13) is an invitation to Jesus' followers to imagine, plead for, and participate in an alternative reality that Jesus identified as the kingdom of God. In contrast to the ruinous and unjust world of first-century Palestine, overseen by the brutal Roman Empire (and indeed in contrast to the brutal empires that rule our times in the twenty-first century), Jesus defines the values of the kingdom as justice, mercy, and righteousness. It is only the "pure in heart [who] will see God" (Matt 5:8).

THE TRANSFIGURATION

The story of the transfiguration is told in the synoptic gospels with minor variations (Matt 17:1–13; Mark 9:2–13; and Luke 9:28–36). As recorded in Scripture, we learn that Jesus took Peter, James, and John with him to a high mountain. The name of the mountain is not mentioned, but is likely to be Mount Hermon, which is adjacent to where he had been teaching. Three wonders took place at the transfiguration. First, Jesus' appearance changed so that his face "shone like the sun, and his clothes became white as the light" (Matt 17:2). Second, Moses and Elijah, two important prophets who were thought to have been long dead, appeared and spoke with Jesus. And third, God spoke saying, "This is my Son, whom I love; with him I am well pleased. Listen to him!" (Matt 17:5).

As this story is most commonly understood, this order of events is without question. The plain sense is that the disciples saw Jesus' appearance change before their very eyes from a natural into a supernatural form, and so they began to understand that Jesus really was who he claimed to be: someone who shared in the very nature of God and who was actively implementing the mission given him by his Father.

However, the Eastern Orthodox theologian Vladimir Lossky has proposed a second possible interpretation of the transfiguration. Following a number of the church fathers, Lossky has proposed that Jesus carried in his human body the glory of his divinity, a glory that had remained unseen by the disciples until they climbed to the top of the mountain. It was only then that Jesus assumed his proper identity, and the disciples were able to see him in his true nature as he always was. "In the Transfiguration, Christ did not become what he was not before, but appeared to his disciples as he was, by opening their eyes, by giving sight to those who were blind."[3] In this understanding what was changed was not Jesus' appearance so much as the disciples' understanding of his identity. On this understanding Jesus did not divest himself of his transcendent and glorious qualities when he was born of the Virgin Mary, but instead simply added humanity to his person, which was already irradiated with light. Finding themselves in the presence of God in human form, the disciples saw Jesus in a different light. More than their friend and spiritual mentor, more than a great religious teacher in the tradition of the Old Testament prophets, more than yet another religious zealot emerging wild-eyed from the Palestinian desert, they understood Jesus to be God's appointed messiah. On Lossky's counter reading of the transfiguration, Peter, who had made the confession, "You are the Christ, the Son of the living God" (Matt 16:16) prior to these events, was now able to understand the full implications of his confession.

It is commonly recognized that Jesus' appearance changed before them, and his face "shone like the sun" (Matt 17:2). However—using Lossky's interpretation as our guide—what is not so widely recognized is that a fourth wonder occurred at the transfiguration; namely, that the disciples themselves underwent a lesser transfiguration in that they saw him in his radiant fullness and were themselves enveloped in the bright cloud and heard God's voice. Understandably, Peter was overwhelmed and uncertain about how to respond, as indeed we would be if we were

3. St. John Damascene, in Lossky, *Vision of God*, 113.

presented with the same situation. On meeting Jesus as he truly was for the first time, the disciples were changed, transformed, even, dare we say, transfigured into his likeness. They too underwent a change in that they recognized Jesus' identity to be the Son of God. Because of their participation in the transfiguration, their vision was changed to the point where they saw Jesus differently, knew Jesus differently, and understood Jesus differently. The disciples' natural senses and their spiritual senses worked together to produce a form of insight, which was the primary work of the mission of Jesus, that lead them to an understanding of his divine sonship. Everyone who truly meets Jesus is transfigured in this way.

THE POWER OF STORY

In his teaching, Jesus broke through the hard surface level of peoples' everyday understandings by employing a form of wisdom language to invite his listeners to both "hear" and "see." In order to awaken his audience's eyes and ears to the spiritual realities that surrounded them, Jesus spoke in the language of story, symbol, poetry, metaphor, and allegory. He told stories about hidden treasure, sheep and goats, pearls of great price, the rich fool, the prodigal son, the lost coin, the master and his servant, building houses, hiding lanterns, and of pouring wine. Each of these stories borrowed scenes from everyday life but infused them with the possibility of new understandings. Inevitably, the new understandings he pointed to required his audience to leave their old convictions and opinions behind, in order for them to arrive at a new perspective on how the world *really* was.

When I was a child my paternal grandmother, Vera, kept some children's books in her laundry cupboard. Whenever I visited her house after school, I would lie on my stomach on her lounge room floor and read. My favorite story was *Puss in Boots*.[4] As I read the story, I found myself unable to remain outside the narrative and was drawn into the storyline as a participant within it. I found myself being drawn into the drama, experiencing the plot tension as if it were a performance that, in some sense, tried to live itself out through me. My imagination was not separate from the drama contained in the story; rather, my whole world was subsumed into the story, and my consciousness became fully

---

4. Written by Charles Perrault (1628–1703), first published in 1697.

engaged with it—making me a participant in the story rather than an outside onlooker. This is the power of story. Jesus, the storyteller, reveals the mystery and the realm of the supernatural through seemingly simple parables. And the story of Jesus reveals the drama of salvation in a personal and compelling way. Fully engaging in this drama personally is the recurring experience of every Christian believer.

The subversive, counterintuitive, threshold stories Jesus told his disciples captured their attention and involved them in a drama that directly addressed their lives. Through plot tension, crisis, and crescendo, they were carried to the brink of resolution—but not quite. Not everything was done to them or for them. They themselves had an important part to play. The disciples were required to choose what response they would make to Jesus. "Who do *you* say I am?" he asked them. (Mark 8:29). Jesus' parabolic teaching called for a radical decision on the part of his listeners; and depending on what decision they made, they either remained wedded to their old way of looking at the world or were enabled to make the imaginative leap to another way of thinking and being. It is there, in that new imaginative space, that they were enabled to find the answers to life's problems, to locate hope where there previously was none, and to encounter the God of grace and mercy to guide them through the uncertainties of life. After having met Jesus and listened to him for a season, it was not possible for them to remain the same. When it comes to Jesus, *believing* is seeing.

It is the nature of story to catch us up into a counter world that our imaginations embrace. Great stories transport and transpose us from our present reality and bring us into the newly discovered world. The story of Jesus is such a story. Whether we like it or not, our human consciousness is set to a default position that prefers story and narrative over dry prescriptive facts. When it comes to story, the stories themselves provide their own background and context, and the reader or listener is given the opportunity to identify their part in the story. By using stories, Jesus was able to get under his listeners' skin, to find ways to challenge what they thought they knew and to transport them to new places—places such as the kingdom of God, places like hope, places like healing, places like salvation—so that they could discover what it was like to be children of light.

SEEING THROUGH JESUS' EYES

The writer Frederick Buechner tells the story of meeting his first grandchild (a grandson) for the very first time. He says what he saw with the eyes in his head "was a very small boy with silvery gold hair and eyes the color of blue denim" coming down the stairs to meet him in his mother's arms. But, as grandfather to the boy, Buechner also saw the child with the eyes of his heart. He saw a little life for whom, without a moment's hesitation, he would willingly give his own life. Grandparents are prone to look at grandchildren like that. They can't get enough of those tiny faces that belong to the precious life in their arms. For Buechner, looking at the child through the eyes of the heart is to see that "every kingdom is magic."[5]

Jesus' call for his hearers to "see with their eyes, hear with their ears, understand with their hearts, and turn," follows a hearing-seeing-understanding-knowing sequence that established an important continuity between the Old Testament and the New Testament accounts of faith.[6] Jesus' call required that worshippers appropriate new spiritual knowledge as a central component of their relationship with God. This theme is heightened in Jesus' ministry, where his practice of using teaching forms that evoked a faith response based on listener insight—revealed by God's Spirit,—ensured that they might "see with their eyes, hear with their ears, understand with their hearts, and turn" (Matt 13:15). In Buechner's words, they were to recognize the presence of the kingdom of God among them. And they were to recognize that they themselves were players in the great drama of salvation history. They were to see through Jesus' eyes, learning to exchange their small kingdoms for his grand kingdom, their sin for his righteousness, their lives for his, their small selfish vision for his universal vision.

The thing about seeing through Jesus' eyes is that we come to the conclusion that Jesus' perspective did not find its origins in some flash of egoistic self-centeredness but out of a God's-eye point of view. As we discussed at the beginning of this chapter, Jesus' self-understanding did not originate from himself but arose out of his filial relationship with his Father through prayer, encounter, and deep discernment. And when Jesus taught the disciples (who were to become his apostles), his intent

---

5. Buechner, *Eyes of the Heart*, 165–66.
6. Watts, *Isaiah 1–33*, 75.

was that they appropriate his Jesus'-eye point of view as their own. And that is what happened. Subsequent to his death, resurrection, and ascension, the apostles began to participate in Jesus' mission to the world. This was not a project of their own imaginings. Their actions are consistent with everything they heard Jesus command them to do. They applied the same point of view they saw Jesus applying. They literally looked through Jesus' eyes rather than their own eyes and saw the magical kingdom of God at work in the world, in them, and through them.

And last of all, those of us who acknowledge ourselves to be followers of Jesus in our own time have appropriated for ourselves the same Jesus'-eye-view perspective that the apostles appropriated for themselves and then preached to the world. This hand-me-down set of understandings is a central feature of Christian discipleship and spirituality, and a requirement for anyone who considers Jesus' question to Peter, "Who do you say that I am?" as being important for their own lives. Peter replied, "You are the Christ, the Son of God" (Luke 9:20). We are to make the same response. It is this confession—which is a comprehensive form of spiritual vision—that marks out the Christian believer from all others.

CONCLUSION

This chapter has explored the Jesus'-eye point of view and the lengths to which Jesus went in his ministry to invite, teach, reveal, provoke, and convince his audience to see eye to eye with him. Ultimately, we have discovered that what matters is not so much what Jesus looked like, but the extent to which those who identify themselves as Jesus' disciples are prepared to look through his eyes. Becoming Jesus' disciples means adopting his vision of life. That vision is best described as the kingdom of God. Of course while we are looking into Jesus' eyes, we need to remember that he is looking into our eyes to determine the extent to which we have understood his call to follow him. Jesus calls us in the times and places where we practice our humanity to see through his eyes. This is not a peripheral task of discipleship; it is the central task of following Christ in an age when many conflicting visions of life compete for our attention.

3

A Visionary Text

"Every eye will see him" (Rev 1:7).

Our task in this chapter is to explore the central role of the Bible in shaping the defining vision of Christian believers. As we will discover, the Bible is a dangerous book; it is a visionary text; it is the sacred Word; and it is a guide through which believers become a "third testament." Indeed, the Bible is a central contributor to shaping the vision of Christian disciples, and without it Christians would lack the language, stories, and points of reference they need to live the Christian spiritual life through their own lives.

A DANGEROUS BOOK

Like all good arcade bookshops these days, the bookshop I shall speak of included a *Body, Mind, and Spirit* section among its other general interest, biography, and fiction offerings. The aforementioned sign drew shoppers' attentions to the religious and spiritual nature of the books standing on the display cabinet. Unintentionally, the sign also conveyed the sense that here were consumer items for sale: the sacred mysteries of dozens of religious traditions conveniently prepackaged and neatly labeled for the Western consumer to buy, and just as quickly discard. Most Westerners want convenience at all costs. That includes, it seems, the supernatural. Red and white labels announced a 20 percent storewide discount, a consequence it seemed of hard financial times. Bizarrely, even the sacred world is made subject to the vagaries of market forces. At the far end of the store, beyond the discounted Dalai Lama, Kabbalah, Shirley MacLaine, and Dr. Phil, a small Christian section could be found. It was stocked with children's Bible stories, trendy prayer books, the current batch of "how to fix your life" paperbacks, and overcooked leadership titles. Several Bibles were stashed so effectively on the lower shelves that one had to bend down to see them. No one seemed to be aware of the danger they presented. I thought to myself, Don't they know these Bibles belong in the brown paper bag section? They should carry a sign: danger, reading this book will change your life! I am always tempted when the airport attendant asks me if I am carrying anything dangerous in my luggage, to say yes—my Bible! The writer Annie Dillard drew attention to the way people consistently underestimate the power of religion and the Bible when she wrote:

> Does anyone have the foggiest idea of what sort of power we so blithely invoke? The churches are children playing on the floor with their chemistry sets, mixing up a batch of TNT to kill a Sunday morning. It is madness to wear ladies' straw hats and velvet hats to church; we should all be wearing crash helmets. Ushers should issue life preservers and signal flares; they should lash us to the pews. For the sleeping God may wake some day and take offense, or the waking God may draw us out where we can never return.[1]

But in the usual quiet hum of the bookshop, no one seemed even vaguely aware that God may awaken or call us out of our spiritual slumber.

The Bible is a book that provokes deep division among people. Among believers, it is the question of interpretation that provokes debate. A theological controversy awaits all who venture an opinion on how best to systematize its contents, which is usually done in terms of the competing perspectives of Calvinism or Arminianism, election or free grace, antinomianism or sinless perfectionism. Among unbelievers, there is uniform skepticism toward the value of the Bible. They argue for its removal from public life, especially as the underwriter of legislation transacted in our houses of government, the education provided in our schools, and as the basis for morality in a pluralist society. Myra Fisher is one such voice who has spoken out to reject the value and authority of the Bible: "If you want humorless, know-it-all men, unbelievable plots, convoluted and often contradictory stories—men living in whales, a jealous God who had favorites and then through the ages punished

---

1. Dillard, *Teaching a Stone to Talk*, 58–59.

them—read the Bible. Like *The Da Vinci Code*, it isn't really believable but it's a bloody good read!"[2]

The Bible is a dangerous book because it divides opinion. It has opinion-dividing power because it has opinion-making power. It also divides people into categories we might think are unhelpful and divisive: sheep and goats, believer and unbeliever, sinner and saint, trustworthy citizen and reprobate. The dividing that occurs in and among people comes as a result of reading its pages. The Bible is a dangerous book. It reminds us that "when you change the way you look at things, the things you look at change."[3]

A VISIONARY TEXT

The Bible is also a visionary text, written by eyewitnesses to bear witness to mystery. Numerous vision narratives are to be found in the Bible. The Old Testament begins with a vision of humankind (Adam and Eve) made in the image of God, dwelling in God's presence in the garden (Gen 1–3). It concludes by looking forward to the "great day of the Lord" in Malachi 4, which anticipates the coming of a great prophet like Elijah who would "turn the hearts of the parents to the children, and the hearts of the children to the parents." Christians believe the one spoken of is Jesus, although he is more than a prophet. Similarly, the New Testament begins with the magi, whose night vision drew them to see the one to whom the guiding star pointed. It concludes with a starburst of visions. First, where "every eye" will see the victorious Christ on his return to earth (Rev 1:7). Second, the exiled apostle John "turn[ed] to see the voice" speaking from behind him, and his vision of the glorious ascended Christ (1:12–20). And third, the vision of a door standing open in heaven and the twenty-four elders and the four living creatures offering worship to God day and night (Rev 4). John's vision amounts to a restatement of Isaiah's vision of God in the temple (Isa 6) and Ezekiel's vision of the glory of God by the river Kebar (Ezek 1). We come to understand that the central figure in each of these unfolding cosmic dramas is Jesus. Finally, the book of Revelation climaxes with the vision of the new heaven and the new earth. The new Jerusalem is

2. Fisher, "Who Are the Letter Writers?" 25.

3. A statement recorded on the front cover of the Australian Christian Blind Mission magazine *Sustainable Change*, Winter 2011. It is originally attributed to Wayne Dyer.

depicted as coming down out of heaven, accompanied by an explanatory voice from the throne saying, "Now the dwelling of God is with men, and he will live with them. They will be his people, and God himself will be their God. He will wipe away every tear from their eyes. There will be no more death or mourning or crying or pain, for the old order of things has passed away" (Rev 21:3–4). It seems the closer you get to heaven, and the closer history comes to its fulfillment, the more reality is "shown."

I want to explore further two vision-soaked accounts from Luke's gospel. I have chosen them because they are great case studies of how important vision is for Christian spirituality. These accounts demonstrate that the New Testament is a visionary text whose primary purpose is to broadcast the story of Jesus in pictorialized form, thus enabling its readers to visualize its storyline even as it is unfolding. The first account is found in the birth narratives in Luke 2. In addition to the visit of the magi, two righteous representatives from historic Judaism happen upon Mary and Joseph as they came to the Jerusalem temple to dedicate the infant Jesus in accordance with Jewish religious requirements.[4] The righteous and devout Simeon—having been informed by the Spirit that he would not die before he had seen God's appointed Messiah—took the infant in his arms and prayed, "Now dismiss your servant in peace. For my eyes have seen your salvation which you have prepared in the sight of all people, a light for revelation to the Gentiles and for the glory of your people Israel" (Luke 2:29–30). This event has become known in Christian liturgy as the Nunc Dimittis (or "Lord now dismiss" in Latin). The other righteous representative, the aged prophetess Anna, gave thanks to God and testified to all those in the vicinity of the temple who were "looking forward to the redemption of Jerusalem" (2:38), concerning God's intentions for the child. God's *showing*, human *seeing*, and the believer's *sanction* are at work in these texts.

The second account is connected with Jesus' post-resurrection appearances to the disciples on the road to Emmaus (Luke 24). This account is well-known and much loved among believers. There are three significant moments here when Jesus revealed himself to his disciples. The accounts are intensely illuminative and visionary. In the first moment, Jesus revealed his true identity to the gathered disciples in the sacramental moment of the breaking of the bread. It was then that "their

---

4. Recounted in Matthew 2:1–12.

eyes were opened and they recognized him" (24:31). In the second moment, Jesus appeared to the gathered disciples, saying "Look at my hands and feet" and "Touch me and see" (24:39). Jesus' desire was to show himself to his disciples. He does so in order to reassure their tremulous faith and to prepare them for the apostolic mission that awaited them. The third moment is when Jesus "opened their minds so they could understand the Scriptures" (24:45) and reminded them of their obligation as witnesses to testify to what they had seen and heard. "Everything must be fulfilled," (24:44) he said. And while he was ascending into heaven, he blessed them. Although it is not stated in the text, this third moment is the culmination of Jesus' ministry among the disciples. It is here that he sealed his impact on them with *one final vision* of himself as the glorious Christ, ascending into heaven to sit at the right hand of God. Through his ascension, Jesus confirmed what the disciples had only understood by faith—that he was in fact the Son of God. This is the moment they would hold in their minds thereafter as they proclaimed the message of the Lordship of Christ across the known world. This vision was Jesus' finale. Their immediate response was to worship him with great joy and to remain in the temple constantly praising God.

THE SCRIPTING NATURE OF SCRIPTURE

Sacred texts such as the Bible exert an astonishing influence on the minds of those who read them. The impact on the reader is larger than we often recognize. In the world that preceded ours, Neanderthal artists entered caves, a burning torch in one hand and a pot of ochre in the other, to record the images that defined their world: hunters and gatherers, bison and buffalo, woolly mammoth and pronghorn antelope, those who worshipped the gods and even the gods themselves in human form. Even in our age—the age of the eye—sacred texts function in a similar way. They inscribe indelible images on the interior consciousness of their readers. Having read the Bible, heard its stories, sung the psalms, prayed the prayers, and encountered Christ in its pages, something happens that shapes the way believers look at the world. The faith community that truly listens to the stories of Scripture comes to confess it, to reenact it, and to interpose their own lives into the text of Scripture and, in turn, read their own existence out of the Scripture. Jim Fodor has suggested that, "By being read, Scriptures work themselves into the lives of the faithful just as yeast is kneaded into dough."[5] Faith communities are in effect the end product of the sacred texts they read. They are, if you will allow it, 3-D representations of what is otherwise a flat text.

Everyone who has even the smallest association with Christianity knows the stories of Jesus walking on water, his healing of the blind man, the feeding of the five thousand, turning water into wine, the crucifixion and resurrection, his ascension into heaven, and his promised second coming. These are the stories of redemption which bring the supernaturalized, transcendental, and otherworldly stuff of heaven into the here and now of the human situation. The biblical scholar Richard Hays calls these stories the "syntax of salvation."[6] They embed believing souls in the sacred world of the biblical drama and provide them with an explanatory system for making sense of their lives in the dual context of their physical selves and their spiritual selves. The Christian story as it is recounted in the Scriptures presents the possibility of God in Christ breaking into the closed, one-dimensional universe of hopelessness and despair, in order to offer hope and wholeness and the possibility of resurrection for those with eyes to see and ears to hear.

According to William Willimon, the Bible exerts a reality-defining power over the church: "Scripture [gives] us a new story, a new narrative account of the way the world was put together, new direction for history, new purpose of being on the earth. The world of Rome had many other stories which gave meaning to people's lives: eroticism, pantheism, polytheism, cynicism. [But] to be a Christian was to be someone who had been initiated, by baptism, into this alternative story of the world . . . Texts like Scripture are *constitutive*, that is, they are busy constituting new worlds."[7]

The reading, memorization, praying, and acting out the substance of the biblical record provides believers with what Bockmuehl calls, "a chain of living memory going back to the apostles themselves" in an unbroken chain of communal and personal recollection.[8] "Scripture records and, in a sense, constitutes [believers'] personal and collective past

---

5. Fodor, "Reading the Scriptures," 141.
6. Hays, *Moral Vision*, 138.
7. Willimon, *Shaped by the Bible*, 21.
8. Bockmuehl, *Seeing the Word*, 184.

and has immense significance in drawing the horizons of their future expectations, hopes, and fears."[9] *If scribes scribe; then Scriptures script.* Scripture acts as a portal into the divine world, populating worshipper's minds with the language, stories, images, events, personalities, types, and archetypes that enable them to cross over from the everyday world of ordinary time and space into sacred time and space.

In Old Testament studies, the idea of the Torah as a portable Sinai that enabled the people of Israel to stand in the place of Moses and see the face of God by proxy is sometimes appealed to. Similarly, the New Testament Scripture provides opportunity for a repeat performance of the founding moments of the Christian community. While readers in subsequent generations were obviously not present in first-century Palestine, the reading and rereading of the biblical narratives enable them to go back to touch and reexperience those founding moments for themselves. Biblical thinking that arises out of the words, person, acts, and redemptive history of Jesus allows Christian believers to get into the flow of redemptive history by experiencing and reexperiencing the life of God in the heart of humankind. The essence of the spiritual life is to reexperience the scriptural realities anywhere at any time, but always according to the received pattern communicated through the biblical narratives.

THE THIRD TESTAMENT

Christians spend a great deal of time and give a great deal of attention to reading the Bible. Worship services are, or should be, given to the reading of the Scriptures. When Christians celebrate, they read the Scriptures; when they mourn, they read the Scriptures. When they look for guidance, they read the Scriptures. Scholars and theologians alike provide tools such as commentaries and reading guides in order to support this foremost activity of the church, in order to promote the reading and understanding of the Scriptures. And this is as it should be, because Christianity is both the product of the Scriptures and the generator of the Scriptures. As a spiritual movement, Christianity has an interdependent relationship with the Bible. Whereas the text of Scripture reads itself into the church, the church reads itself out of the Scripture.

---

9. Biderman, *Scripture & Knowledge*, 9.

But having said that—for Protestants at least—it is the Scripture that has priority over the community that reads it. In this way the Scripture provides a series of personalized narratives that may once have been events in history; but because of the generalizability of story, poetry, art, and narrative they have become particularized into the stories of every reader, in every place, and in every time. As Bockmuehl informs us, Scripture appears to expect a certain kind of reader—which he calls an *implied reader*—who has through crisis and encounter, transformation and recognition "undergone a religious, moral and intellectual conversion to the gospel of which the documents speak. Regardless of whether the texts instruct, narrate, or reprove, they implicitly assume that the readers share a stance of Christian faith, that they look to the Christian gospel as formative and normative in their lives, and that they accept a Christian way of thinking about God, the world, and themselves."[10]

However, it is possible, perhaps even necessary, for believers to go beyond the notion of an implied reader to the idea of an implied actor who "goes and does likewise" (Luke 10:37) by embodying the life of Jesus in their own lives, thus making us third testaments.

Malcolm Muggeridge (1903–1990) was a British social critic and atheist turned Catholic Christian who developed the idea of the Christian believer as a "third testament."[11] Muggeridge served with the British spy agency MI6 in espionage operations on the continent during the Second World War. Upon returning to England after the war, he lived a libertine life and was known for his acerbic wit and cynical spirit. However, he became a Christian at age 83. He was a household name across England, becoming affectionately known as St. Mugg. In order to better understand the faith he now confessed, he selected a group of influential Christians for careful analysis (St. Augustine, Blaise Pascal, William Blake, Søren Kierkegaard, Leo Tolstoy, and Dietrich Bonhoeffer). Each of these men was influential in (Western) Christian history and was likely to have been influential in his own coming to faith. But Muggeridge reserved special respect for Mother Teresa of Calcutta, whose efforts on behalf of the poor deeply moved him. He wrote of her: "Mother Teresa is, in herself, a living conversion; it is impossible to be

---

10. Bockmuehl, *Seeing the Word*, 70.
11. Muggeridge, *Third Testament*, 1977.

with her, to listen to her, to observe what she is doing and how she is doing it, without being in some degree converted."[12]

In Muggeridge's understanding, the Old Testament was the first testament, the New Testament was the second testament, and the lives of these men in particular and of Christians in general represented the third testament. In referring to Christians as "testaments" Muggeridge was not breaking new ground. He had biblical support for the idea. The apostle Paul made reference to the gospel of Jesus being written on the hearts of his readers and listeners when he wrote to the church in Corinth: "You are a letter from Christ, the result of our ministry, written not with ink but with the Spirit of the living God, not on tablets of stone but on tablets of human hearts" (2 Cor 3:3). Because of the scripting effect of the Scripture, an enduring deposit of faith is impressed onto the consciousness of the believer—somewhat like a coin-stamping machine stamping its imprint on raw metal or a software program rewriting an existing computer program. Fodor's idea, as noted in the previous section, is that through being read the Scriptures work themselves into the lives of the faithful. This idea explains the scripting influence of Scripture on the lives of Christian believers. The biblical story overwrites the readers' existing cultural and personal knowledge and leaves a deposit of faith knowledge imprinted in their inner-worlds. There is a word for this—*palimpsest*. A palimpsest is a piece of chalkboard or parchment where what was previously written has been erased and overwritten by a new narrative that now defines the reader's world. This new faith knowledge contains an awareness of Christ sourced from the scriptural texts, which is the result of Christians reading and rereading the Bible until they come to indwell a world which is imbued with biblical qualities and possibilities. Those possibilities are filled with the presence of angels and demons, diseases and miracles, bondage and delivery, lostness and foundness, alienation and salvation. Because Christians have adopted biblical language, and the biblical thought forms have become ingrained in their belief systems and plausibility structures, they in fact become walking Bibles, little *christs*, ambassadors of another world—even as they continue to live in this world. Christians are walking palimpsests who carry in their inner consciousness the biblical script that overwrites whatever was written before and replaces it with a new redemptive and supernatural narrative.

12. Muggeridge, *Conversion*, 15.

I think Muggeridge was right to draw attention to the Christian believing soul being the third testament. But what is missing among Christian believers, and anyone interested in understanding their faith world, is the lack of any apparatus for understanding and interpreting the subjectivity of spiritual faith found within the interiorized world of the believer. Many helpful tools have been developed for understanding how to read the Bible, but few (if any) tools have been developed for how to read and understand the results of the Bible's impact on the lives of real people in real time. I argue here that developing a greater understanding of the believing soul as a form of third testament is a priority for Christian saints and servants who are concerned with reproducing the substance of the biblical narratives in the lives of believers through spiritual formation, spiritual direction and spiritual education, among others.

The first thing to be said is that Bockmuehl's *implied readers* of the Bible are very aware of the change of outlook and perspective that has occurred in their lives as a consequence of reading the Bible and undergoing the conversion experience. These readers are aware there is a new foundation for their lives, which has originated from the biblical text and now exerts itself upon and through their lives. An outstanding example of people who have found themselves being changed by what they read in the Bible is found in Bernard of Clairvaux (1090–1153) who said, "I went into the higher part of myself, and higher still I found the Kingdom of the Word. Impelled by curiosity to explore still further, I descended deep into myself, and yet I found him deeper still. I looked outside, and met him far beyond everything exterior to me. I looked within; he is more inward than I myself. And I recognize the truth of what I had read, that we live and move and have our being in him."[13]

Bernard is only too aware that the reading of the Bible had produced a change within himself, and so he set out on an interior quest to read the changes in himself that his reading of the Bible had produced.

The second thing to be said is that if there is an agreed approach to the reading of the Bible, there ought also to be an agreed approach to the reading of the saint. It is generally agreed that when reading the text of the Bible, the contemporary reader ought to give particular attention to identifying the author (the source), the recipients (the target audience), the context (the historical situation), the message (the content of

---

13. St Bernard, *Cantica*, Sermon 74, 97.

the communication), and beyond that the significance of the text for his or her own life as a word from God. But there is no agreed approach to interpreting the inner life of the saint or to identifying the enduring vision at the heart of Christian belief. It is at least as necessary for the observer of today's saints to identify what the believing soul knows, sees, and understands about God, the world, and themselves (in response to reading the Scriptures and interpreting the everyday world) as it is for observers to understand the non-Christian's response to the same objects and trigger points, and the meanings and interpretations they generate. Although it may sound heretical to some Protestant readers, I now understand why Roman Catholic and Orthodox believers place next to their Bible a Book of Saints. Both books elaborate on the spiritual life, but do so in different yet complementary ways.

The third thing to be said is that since the Bible is the most widely sold and read book in the Western world, we would be naive to expect that it would fail to exert an influence on the psyches of those people who read it. Even the atheist Richard Dawkins argues for the retention of the Bible in Western society. He waxes lyrical on the outstanding literary merits of the 1611 King James Bible and the sublimity of the wisdom of the Song of Songs and Ecclesiastes. Whether or not he has actually understood what he has read is another thing. But the list of sayings that Dawkins identified has made its way from the text of the Bible into everyday parlance:

> Be fruitful and multiply; am I my brother's keeper?; the fat of the land; stranger in a strange land; burning bush; let my people go; fleshpots; an eye for an eye and a tooth for a tooth; be sure your sin will find you out; the apple of his eye; Shibboleth; a man after his own heart; how are the mighty fallen!; the wisdom of Solomon; girding up his loins; the patience of Job; escaped by the skin of his teeth; to everything there is a season, and a time for every purpose; the race is not to the swift, nor the battle to the strong; the wolf also will dwell with the lamb, and the leopard shall lie down with the kid; get behind me Satan; the salt of the earth; turn the other cheek; wolf in sheep's clothing; new wine in old bottles; crumbs from the table; wars and rumors of wars; good and faithful servant; separate the sheep from the goats; suffer the little children; the widow's mite; physician heal thyself; the good Samaritan; the lost sheep; the prodigal son; cast the first stone; through a glass darkly; all flesh is as grass; fight the good fight; I am the Alpha and the Omega; Armageddon.[14]

14. Dawkins, *God Delusion*, 341–43.

Although Dawkins wishes only to retain the Bible for its literary merit—acknowledging that "the atheistic worldview provides no justification for cutting the Bible, and other sacred books, out of our education"—he argues strongly against those people who read it "as if it were true," arguing that the Bible should be removed from the educational curriculum of schools.[15] He reasons that to expose children to the stories of the Bible is an act of child abuse, firstly on the grounds that it represents an ideological act and secondly on the grounds that it removes their right to make choices about their beliefs for themselves. But Dawkins is either unwilling or unable to apply the same logic to the atheist Sunday schools he later goes on to describe—and promote. The idea that biblical epistemology is ideological but atheist epistemology is value free is laughable. From the point of view of the Christian believing soul, the Bible forms not only the center of the faith they have come to profess but forms the personal and communal identity that now defines their existence. They are now the owners of an outlook that is God soaked, redemption centered, and supernaturally focused.

CONCLUSION

The theme that has repeatedly come to the fore in this chapter is the extent of the scripting nature of Scripture, shaping as it does the vision of Christian disciples, and that without it Christians would lack the language, stories, guidance, and reference points they need to participate in the spiritual life. From the perspective of the believing soul, the narratives of salvation that fill the pages of the Bible offer a new foundation on which to establish their lives. These foundations are absorbed into the internal operating system of the mind of the believer and function in his or her everyday life through a circle of awareness:

> *See* and know,
> Know and be,
> Be and do,
> Do and *see*,
> *See* and know etc.[16]

---

15. Ibid., 344.
16. Pike, "On the Emics and Etics," 45.

4

A Wide-Eyed People

"We saw the glory with our own eyes" (John 1:14, *The Message*).

OUR TASK IN THIS chapter is to identify the enduring vision that shapes the identity and informs the worship life of the church as the confessing community. Our goal is to come to understand how the faithful know what they know, and what is it that makes them capable of seeing the glory of Christ with their own eyes? My goal in this chapter is to help you look through the eye of faith of the Christian community to see what the community sees and to read the world through the interpretive lens that community wears. Using the language of Christians as a wide-eyed people will help us in our inquiries.

THE INTERPRETIVE COMMUNITY

Some people think Christians are crazy. It has become routine in the Western world for religious belief to be treated as a sign of weakness or even mental illness. Sigmund Freud, the father of psychoanalysis, suggested that religious belief was the result of an illusion in the mind. More recently, the atheist philosopher Richard Dawkins has suggested that those holding religious beliefs go beyond being simply illusional to being delusional. Portrayals of Christians in the media are consistently derogatory. They are depicted by worldly wise and fad-savvy critics as fundamentalist killjoys, God-botherers, and moral tightwads whose preoccupations with family values and conservative politics ensure they are typecast to represent the worst form of dogmatism, unreasonableness, and sacrosanct prudishness. The famed openness of the Western liberal spirit appears to falter and fail when it comes to presenting authentic religious practices and experiences in a sensitive and tolerant manner. Instead of reporting Christian beliefs in an unbiased and professional fashion, the media often misrepresents Christian spirituality and those who practice it. In any case, some people think Christians are crazy.

This is not new. Jesus himself was accused of being "out of his mind" (Mark 3:21) and "raving mad" (John 10:20). And the apostle Paul was labeled by King Agrippa as someone who was "out of [his] mind" (Acts 26:24). What is at stake here is not mental disease or so-called insanity, but the ability to recognize a form of changed religious belief that has become deeply etched on the consciousness of those who confess Christ. The confession of a new believer is not madness but is to them the most obvious form of sanity.

On any given Sunday morning around the world, Christians gather to worship Jesus Christ as God. The places where they meet for worship might be a traditional church building or an open-air park, an industrial warehouse or a suburban home, an isolated farm shed or a high-rise penthouse. Once gathered, they hear the reading of Scripture, pray their prayers, confess the creeds, participate in the Eucharist, and baptize the new (either as infants or as adult believers). It may not look like it but these activities, when rightly understood, can be as revolutionary as any Marxist political meeting or any terrorist recruiting exercise.

The biblical scholar Walter Brueggemann imagines a typical Sunday morning, with a typical Christian congregation sitting in their pews, awaiting the preacher to announce the morning's text. On this particular morning the Scriptures are read and the sermon is preached. The preacher stands in front of the congregation, which has in their minds two worlds—this earthly world and the new heavenly world—and all the preacher has in his or her hands is what appears to be an old, odd, outdated hoary text.[1] The three-point sermon traditionally speaks of (1) sin, (2) redemption, and (3) new life in Christ. Behind the traditional formulas and ritual activities there lies a world of meaning. Upon hearing the preacher's stumbling attempts to unpack the biblical narrative, the attentive, listening, and confessing Christian community is transported out of its presumed, taken-for-granted world and—whether they know it or not, whether they like it or not—are transported out of their old assumptions about money, sex, power, and possessions and brought into a new proposed world where everything takes on a God-shaped hue. Just

---

1. Brueggemann, *Texts Under Negotiation*, 22.

as Doctor Who's Tardis contains in its telephone box space a vast inner geography that houses the good Doctor's equipment and enables him to travel to unknown destinations, so too the church's Sunday worship (which involves the telling and retelling of the biblical story) opens out to swallow up the ordinary world.

When *creation* is read out of the Scriptures and taught in the church, believers accept it by faith as belonging to the new reality of the kingdom of God on which the entire physical and spiritual world is founded. Creation is not understood as a bookish doctrine but as the only possible explanation for the way things are in the world. When *election* is read out of the Scriptures and taught in the church, believers become aware that God has chosen them and made them his own dearly loved children; and so they are convinced that they now have a new name and a place to belong in the bosom of God. The world in which they live switches from one that is a random and meaningless existence into an existence filled with purpose and significance. When *salvation* is read out of the Scriptures and taught in the church, it is not mere dogma. On the contrary, it becomes the primary interpretive formula from which everything else takes its perspective. In salvation, God reached down in Christ, and in an act of ultimate mercy and grace, relieved the guilt and suffering of humanity overloaded with depravity and sin. Such is the power of the idea of salvation that it is the centerpiece of the entire Christian story. When *sanctification* and the holy life are read out of the Scriptures and taught in the church, the believing community makes Christ's crucifixion the stimulus towards living a holy and righteous life. And when the *last things* are read out of the Scriptures and taught in the church, there is an expectation of the coming-soon return of Christ to judge his enemies and to reward his saints in an impending moment in history. It is the nature of eschatology to look beyond the mere appearances of the outward world to see a hope that cannot be seen with the human eye. Such counter realities are only seen through the eye of faith. And what the eye of faith reads in the mystery of God's purposes and promises is what the theologians call salvation history, where a biblically-shaped God's-eye-view reading of history interprets the ordinary everyday material world through the lens of God's intentions and actions. That is why Christians consistently care for the sick, feed the hungry, clothe the poor, have compassion on the needy and rescue the lost. Why? Because as a wide-eyed people whose vision is filled with an understanding of God's purposes for his fallen world, they change earthly linear time to supernatural redemptive time. For the Christian community, heaven has already come to earth.

The state of mind of Christian believers is obviously not that of the demented and the insane. Who else in history has cared for the sick, fed the hungry, clothed the poor, had compassion on the needy and rescued the lost? No, Christians are not *out* of their minds; but it is undeniable that they have Christ *in* their minds. Christians have within them a new mind that prompts them to operate out of a fundamentally different hermeneutic from that of their critics. The state of mind of the Christian faith community is, by all accounts, admittedly an alternate or even an altered state of mind, but it is not an illusional or even a delusional state of mind. Rather, the church is a physical and social extension of the narrative world of Scripture (as discussed in the previous chapter). In the final analysis, the most significant source of a Christian's perception (that is, their thinking, seeing, knowing, and acting) arises out of his or her encounter with God in Christ, the possibility and precedent for which is found in the biblical narratives. Christians are not wild-eyed bigots who need to be locked away in mental wards. Christians are wide-eyed people who have in their minds two worlds—this earthly world, which is passing away, and the new heavenly world, which is eternal. Our task as Christians is always to interpret the one to the other. We interpret heaven to earth through mission and evangelism; and we interpret earth to heaven through prayer and acts of justice and compassion.

PARTICIPATIVE KNOWING

For the most part our schools, colleges, and universities have adopted a one-dimensional view of reality and thus are only able to teach people how to measure, assess, and count objects in the material world. As such, coming to understand the Christian point of view is not an easy task for a generation of people who have been educated in this authorized version of right-mindedness. Interestingly, the kinds of language and measures that skeptical reason is capable of producing are not competent to recognize or assess spiritual entities, let alone to describe or interact with them. So, talk of spiritual knowing is not an easy task for citizens of the twenty-first century trained in the art of empirical thinking. But in the changed circumstances that confront us in the post-9/11, post-

GFC (global financial crisis), and post-sustainable world in which we live, new forms of knowing and new ways of seeing the world can now be safely explored. These new ways of seeing include a willingness to explore new forms of consciousness, including the spiritual life and what the spiritual believer knows, sees, and believes.

With the help of philosophers such as Michael Polanyi, we have come to realize that human knowledge is always personal knowledge. This knowledge is not so much cognitive and rationalistic (i.e., stuck in the mind) as we have come to think; rather it is much more prereflective, assumptive, and taken for granted (i.e., held in the whole person: body, mind, and spirit). Spiritual knowledge especially is like that. Such knowing "is less about information and more about transformation; less about comprehension and more about being apprehended."[2] This does not mean, of course, that we leave our brains at the door when we talk about spiritual things. On the contrary, C. S. Lewis calls us to attention with the following statement: "If you are thinking of becoming a Christian, I warn you you are embarking on something which is going to take the whole of you, brains and all. But fortunately, it works the other way round. Anyone who is honestly trying to be a Christian will soon have his intelligence being sharpened: one of the reasons why it needs no special education to be a Christian is that Christianity is an education itself. That is why an uneducated believer like Bunyan was able to write a book that has astonished the whole world."[3]

But the kind of knowledge that is embedded in spiritual knowing is whole-person knowledge, uniting our rational and emotive, embodied and interrelational ways of knowing. Such knowledge extends beyond the mind's capacity to grasp fully, even if it can develop rational arguments for or against such knowledge. But spiritual knowing includes such things as allegiance, defining commitments, and deep-seated emotional attachments that define a person's identity and life direction. As Blaise Pascal (1623–1662) stated, "The heart has reasons that reason cannot know."[4] But those reasons frequently provide the starting point for a person's, or indeed an entire community's way of being in the world. If we are open to the universe, we will want to explore these reasons, even if we constantly find ourselves falling short of complete understanding.

2. Meek, *Loving to Know*, 2011, in a summary on the back cover of the book.
3. Lewis, *Mere Christianity*, 71.
4. Pascal, *Pensées*, 154.

I have discovered that one of the most meaningful ways of talking about spiritual knowing is something called "participative knowing." The authors Ferrer and Sherman explore what they call the "participatory turn" in spirituality, mysticism, and religious studies.[5] They are careful not to define participatory knowing too closely, lest they unnecessarily constrain its meaning. Using some of the concepts provided by Ferrer and Sherman, I want to explore participatory knowing further.[6]

1. Participatory knowing is a concept capable of engaging with spiritual knowing. It goes beyond the ability of standard forms of biological and reductionist descriptions to account for the dynamic and nonreducible nature of the visionary imagination so central to religious commitment and spiritual experience. Participatory knowing helps us to locate concepts and language better suited to the invisible spirit energies and ways of knowing that are a part of spiritual experience. Participatory knowing helps us make sense of spiritual experience.

2. Participatory knowing is multidimensional and true to life. It is open to spiritual meaning and experience, and recognizes its "participatory, connected, and often passionate" modes of experiencing, knowing, and being.[7] It recognizes that context plays an important role in the acquisition and production of knowledge, including the relational and interpersonal aspects central to spiritual knowing.

3. Participatory knowing brings together inward commitment and outward action. People of faith are not happy to leave things as they are. They want to remake the world in the image and likeness of heaven. Ferrer uses the term *enaction* to describe the saints' "working with" the supernatural reality they encounter in their imaginative faith vision to remake reality according to the model they have seen in the sacred realm.[8] Authentic spirituality is not simply a passive inward-directed phenomena, but seeks to engage the world head-on in the spirit of the Lord's Prayer, (e.g., "Your will be done on earth").

5. Ferrer and Sherman, *Participatory Turn*, 2008.
6. Ibid., 55, 72.
7. Ferrer, "Spiritual Knowing," 137.
8. Ibid., 136–37.

4. Participatory knowing applies especially to the Christian faith. Participatory knowledge applies directly to Christian experience and spiritual knowing. While the participatory turn can apply to any experience—secular or religious—we argue here that it has particular relevance to Christian spirituality. Bruno Barnhart[9] maneuvers to "retrieve the participatory Christian vision" by identifying the concept of participation as a hermeneutical key "which promises to open our common history . . . to a new depth of understanding."[10] He argues that the Christian faith is built upon the notion of participation. Jesus participates in the Father's divine identity and invites his disciples to participate in his own life as members of the kingdom of God through divinization. Barnhart cites the Apostle Paul's words, "Is not the cup of thanksgiving for which we give thanks a *participation* in the blood of Christ? And is not the bread that we break a *participation* in the body of Christ?" (1 Cor 10:16, my italics). In this way, Barnhart argues that Christianity is above all else a participatory faith.

When the Christian believer contemplates the person of Jesus—the One whom they love—their mode of knowing and relating to him conforms to a participatory way of knowing, that is, whole person, interactive, and perceptive.

Esther Meek is a Christian writer who has reflected on participatory knowing at length.[11] Meek explores participatory knowing using the two concepts of *knowing* and *loving*. It should not surprise us that loving and knowing are close friends. The medieval theologian, William of Saint Thierry wrote, "The love of God is our knowledge of him."[12] Simone Weil wrote, "Love is the soul's looking. It means that we have stopped for an instant to wait and listen."[13] And the philosopher Paul Ricoeur observed that "love gives rise to thought."[14] Meek calls the connction-

---

9. Barnhart, "One Spirit, One Body," 265–91.
10. Ibid., 266.
11. Meek, *Loving to Know*, 2011.
12. Merton, *Seven Storey Mountain*, 204.
13. Weil, *Waiting for God*, 140.
14. Discussed in Olthius, *Knowing Otherwise*, 244.

between loving and knowing "covenant epistemology."[15] Placing the two words *covenant* (agreement) and *epistemology* (the foundations of knowledge) together, Meek presents a convincing case that loving God is like falling in love. The kinds of whole-of-life commitments and deeply felt meanings that apply to our most superlative human experiences are the same as those we experience as a matter of course in our spiritual lives. The affairs of the human heart, falling in love, and the deeply convincing nature of spiritual experience are all directly related. That is why Meek's statement, "knowing is less about information and more about transformation; less about comprehension and more about being apprehended"[16] is so important. Only the concept of falling in love is big enough to capture the experience of a human person caught up "in the act" of spiritual encounter. There is a certain kind of absolute surrender that occurs when a person gives their life to Christ, and it can only be compared to an intense kind of falling in love.

As is the case with Ferrer and Sherman's work, I will explore the topic of spiritual knowing using Meek's idea of "covenant epistemology." Her work describes the kinds of deep-seated, relationship-based, convictional knowledge that is a central feature of the Christian spiritual experience.

1. All knowing is personal knowing. Knowledge, or our mode of being in a relationship with an object or person, is only possible if it is possessed by a knower. The Cartesian epistemology of a disembodied mind attempts to give priority to some sort of universally accessible truth. But objects in themselves do not have knowledge; knowledge must be generated and held by persons who are centers of conscious existence. All knowledge is knowledge by someone. Despite the fact that human knowing is imperfect and we do not always get it right, the extent to which we are capable of knowing is potentially near complete knowledge: "Our efforts to know are fallible but also quite capable, *coram Deo*[17] and in God's world, of leading us to the truth. Our humanness serves as a beachhead within reality."[18] Christians would say

---

15. Meek, *Loving to Know*, 395–423.
16. Meek, *Loving to Know*, from book summary on the back cover.
17. Meaning "living before the face of God."
18. Meek, *Loving to Know*, 410.

we do not know everything; but we know enough from the signs of providence and the world around us, from the Scriptures, and from our encounter with Christ to want to place ourselves in a right relationship with God. Human knowers "differ from the divine Knower" by reason of their place in the scheme of things.[19] God knows everything there is to be known, including his human subjects. We, on the other hand, know only in a contingent and conditional way. One sign of the smallness of our knowing is that it must be constantly renewed—hence a lifetime of studying the Bible is preferable to reading it only once. To that extent we do not know something completely, but find ourselves knowing in a fumbling yet still reliable way. In that process we ourselves come to be known. The mystery of our existence as human persons makes sense when we discover that we are loved by God completely and that our lives in the everyday material world are the places where that love is most clearly expressed. All knowledge is personal—including spiritual knowledge—and is expressed *through* and embodied *in* the human person.

2. All knowing is relational in nature. Covenantal epistemology suggests that knowledge cannot be possessed by a solitary knower. Knowledge is always reciprocal and expresses a unique form of intimacy. The knower himself or herself is given an understanding of *the real*, disclosed in a moment of elevated awareness. There is a certain intimacy about knowing that enables the Christian disciple (for example) to understand things that belong intersubjectively to the persons of God or Jesus Christ, but which have been made known to us through God's loving self giving. "Truth is troth," as Meek puts it.[20] Only in the context of personal commitment and personal disclosure is it possible to truly encounter someone—including the divine *Someone*. "Lovers make great knowers," says Meek.[21] To that extent, all knowing is knowing *with* another person, whether human or divine.

---

19. Ibid., 409–10
20. Ibid., 406.
21. Ibid., 400.

3. All knowing is embedded knowing. Knowing is deeply connected to the cultural, social, linguistic, and relational environment in which it takes place. David Kettle draws attention to the contextual nature of all knowing.[22] He says all forms of knowing are rooted in the context that surrounds the knower and creates the conditions for knowing. A person or community's culture and narrative history provides the circle of possibilities that frame and inform the thought lives of those who believe. Kettle argues that humans "inhabit a world-context. . . . With respect to our most fundamental, lively, personal knowledge, our context denotes the world that we actively, practically inhabit in our knowing, and *this act of inhabiting a world-context is integrally part of the act of knowing itself.*"[23] From a Christian perspective, God makes himself known to us through the life contexts provided by our culture, language, gender, ethnicity, and set of relations. All knowledge is *embedded knowledge.* The circle of possibilities provided by our enframing context includes the set of stories we live amongst. Sometimes, in order to find meaning and truthfulness in our lives, we have to oppose and resist the authorized version of right-mindedness that surrounds us (e.g., consumerism and hyperindividualism). At other times, in order to find meaning and truthfulness in our lives, we have to transcend the stories handed down to us by our ancestors (e.g., when a child whose parents are culture-Christians [i.e., in name only] becomes a real Christian by meeting Christ for herself). While all knowing is context specific, we as Christians would argue that we are not bound by our context, and that coming to believe in Christ provides us with a larger and more habitable context than we are given in our limited human situation.

4. All knowing is *participative* knowing. So we return to where we began by saying that all knowing is participatory knowing and, in particular, that spiritual knowing requires the use of the whole person: mind, body, spirit, conscience, memory, anticipation, relationship, and love. In this way all knowing is *knowing through* the sensing faculties given to us. Meek writes of "inviting

---

22. Kettle, *Western Culture*, 45–47.
23. Ibid., 46. Author's italics.

the real," through which she seeks to facilitate a drawing near to the mysterious but surprisingly recognizable face of God in the world. For Meek it is in the context of relationship that a form of therapy can be applied. This therapy offers to fix the defective or default knowing of the authorized version of right-mindedness. Participatory knowing is about launching out on a quest to seek for something one knows is there but cannot, for the moment, identify. This something can only be found by launching out with the whole self to find the pearl of great price, in Christ, which is the fulfillment of the deepest longings of the human heart.

So let us say, in summary, that the Christian church is a wide-eyed community because it is attentive to those forms of knowing that enable it to truly see God. It opens itself to the truthfulness of the biblical narrative by listening with the ear of the soul. And having heard the cadences of heaven, the ear is turned into a spiritual eye where everything comes into view and what is seen is loved, and what is loved is seen. As Meek says: "I believe that seeing, as a human activity, actually can be and must be redeemed, recast so that it is thought of as a sort of visual touch, one that evokes mutuality and reciprocity. For there is a kind of seeing that distances us from the object; there is a kind of seeing that moves beyond objectifying and allows us to see from the inside out. (Think of the word, *insight*). There is also a kind of seeing which we rightly call vision, in which we sense possibilities and significances hitherto overlooked."[24]

This is why the writer Annie Dillard can tell us that, "The lover can see, and the knowledgeable";[25] and why C. S. Lewis can say that "the instrument through which you see God is your whole self."[26]

CHRIST PLAYS IN TEN THOUSAND LIVES

Eugene Peterson, pastor, theologian, and writer of *The Message*,[27] wrote a book entitled *Christ Plays in Ten Thousand Places*.[28] In it he describes how Christ plays or acts out his redemptive drama through his church in

---

24. Meek, *Loving to Know*, 26.
25. Dillard, *Pilgrim at Tinker Creek*, 29.
26. Lewis, *Mere Christianity*, 140.
27. Peterson, *The Message*, 1996.
28. Peterson, *Christ Plays in Ten Thousand Places*, 2005.

multitudinous places and ways. Peterson borrows heavily from Gerard Manley Hopkins' sonnet "As Kingfishers Catch Fire," from which he takes the line "for Christ plays in ten thousand places" to become the title of his book. Peterson invites us to reflect on the possibility that amidst the world of chaos and despair that surrounds us, we catch glimpses of Christ's goodness playing out in the lives of ordinary Christians who manifest Christ to the world through their acts of kindness to others. How does Christ do this? Through his "lovely limbs" (think of the "beautiful feet" of Isa 52:7 and Rom 10:15); through his "lovely eyes not his" (here the image of the eye of faith comes into focus); and through the "features of men's faces" (here are the reflections of Christ's visage in the faces of his disciples, male and female).[29]

I recently discovered a helpful metaphor that brings these ideas into focus even more clearly, while I was listening to my car radio. The commentator interviewed a teacher from the School of the Air in Australia.[30] Because of the vastness of the Australian outback and the sparse population that lives there, no other form of education is practicable.[31] Educating children across the vast distances of central Australia presents a unique challenge. Apart from sending children to boarding schools in capital cities or regional towns, education through technology is the only real option. Radio and Internet classes provided through the School of the Air are an effective means of educating children who live on outback farms and stations.

The radio interview I heard described how the annual Christmas play was rehearsed and performed. The script for the Christmas play was chosen by the teacher then sent to students by e-mail. The students familiarized themselves with the script of the play they were to "perform." When the day of the performance arrived, the students remained in their usual locations on their outback farms and stations, but they took part in the play as a living drama over the airwaves—to the delight of the students, their teachers, and family members listening in.

---

29. Ibid., 3.

30. For further information on the School of the Air see http://australia.gov.au/about-australia/australian-story/school-of-the-air.

31. An estimated 0.03 people per square kilometer live in Australia's outback, compared with an average of 2 people per square kilometer for the total population in the remainder of the country.

This example gives a rough approximation of how the Christian church lives its life and does its faith as a corporate community, regardless of the time or place in which it resides. Because the church shares a common consciousness and a unifying story centered on the person of Jesus, the life of Christ is made evident through the lives of Christian disciples scattered across the far corners of the planet. It is there—in the tens of thousands, or in fact hundreds of millions, of lives who have been touched by the life of Christ—that the Christian story is envisioned, participated in, and acted out. The believing community's act of listening to the biblical drama means they do not simply become actors in a play that does not belong to them. Rather, they become wide-eyed participants in a reality that takes its lead from the biblical script and which—through transformative engagement, participatory knowing, and covenantal epistemology—becomes the means by which Christ plays out his script in the world through their lives. It is not so much that these people have lost their lives to some despotic cult; rather it is more that they have found a cause that completes their humanness and, for the first time in their lives, has given them something truly worth living and dying for.

CONCLUSION

In this chapter we have sought to come to an understanding of the enduring vision that lies at the center of the Christian faith, and the mode of knowing that is central to the Christian spiritual life. We have described Christians as something other than a bunch of crazy lunatics, but rather as a community of wide-eyed people who "look through" a Christ-centered interpretive paradigm that has become their worldview or interpretive lens. That lens has at its center a creational, redemptive, and transformative hermeneutic. Christians are not mad, bad, or sad—they are a global community for whom the Jesus'-eye point of view has become the defining idea.

Our inquiries in this chapter have prepared us for the topic of the next chapter: the kingdom of light.

5

The Kingdom of Light

"In your light we see light" (Ps 36:9).

OUR TASK IN THIS chapter is to inquire into the illuminative nature of the Christian faith. References to light are featured in many of Jesus' teachings and shine out from every corner of the New Testament. Light is a central image in Christian worship and makes its presence felt in Christian spiritual knowing. The goal in this chapter is to explore the connection between the enduring vision that lies at the center of Christian spiritual experience—and light.

THE LIGHT OF CHRIST

At the front of the Methodist church where I worshipped with my family for the first twenty years of my life is a stained-glass window that depicts a life-sized image of Jesus. He stands with a crimson cloak draped over his shoulders and he faces the congregation. His right hand is raised in a sign of greeting. The greeting can be read as the risen Christ bestowing a blessing on his friends and followers. In his left hand he holds a lantern that radiates light. The words, "I am the light of the world" (John 8:12) are inscribed across the window. This pictorial gospel signifies that Jesus is the bringer of light, both for his people and for the whole world. I can remember myself as a small boy sitting in the congregation and staring up into that face. That face emitted a luster and a confidence that has left an indelible impression on me even to this day. The face of Jesus has been a subject on which I have reflected deeply throughout my life. My understanding then, as now, is that Jesus is God's light bearer and the one who offers illumination to his people.

The theme of Jesus as the bringer of light and the bestower of the kingdom of light is one that has exerted an intense shaping influence on the Christian faith from its earliest beginnings. Light is a theme basic to Christianity. Light originates from the person of God himself as an attribute of the Divine person (i.e., "God *is* light" [1 John 1:5]) and from whose being radiates a brilliant form of light. God himself is the source of light. Light emanates outwards from God throughout the whole of creation. And light completes its journey in the person of Jesus who said, "I am the light of the world" (John 8:12). In making its journey from heaven to earth, light loses none of its incandescence. God's light and Jesus' light are one and the same. Like love, light is an essential theological theme because it both finds its origin in the being of God and flows out through the divine attributes into the created order. The making of light was one of God's first acts in creation when he formed the sun and moon. They are to endure as long as the earth endures, signifying God's beneficence over all he has made. Light is also the sign of God's approval toward all people, including his own special people. In this way light becomes a manifestation of divine life that radiates throughout the created order, and a symbol of God's life, goodness, and salvation. But light is not limited to the act of creation; it also shines in redemption. People who experience the salvation made available through faith in Christ are able to participate in the light of Christ as their (second) birthright. If we are excited about St. Elmo's fire or the Northern lights, then there is even more reason to be excited about the light that Christ brings.

Light and sight are primary features of the spiritual life, as is shown by the light versus darkness and sight versus blindness metaphors that pervade the Bible. If we are to fully understand the concept of light in the Christian spiritual life, we must first take note of two significant warnings. The first warning is that when we draw near to God there is an excess of light. The biblical description of God is that he "dwells in unapproachable light" (1 Tim 6:16) and therefore cannot be seen as he is in himself by the naked human eye. The idea that pervades the Old Testament is that no one can see God and live (Ex 33:20). Here we are confronted with the Jewish understanding of Yahweh's utter holiness. That is why he separates himself from sinful humankind. God hides himself from humanity and refuses to give his glory to anyone else (Ps 42:8). That is why Isaiah cried out: "Woe to me! I am ruined! For I am a man of unclean lips . . . and my eyes have seen the King, the Lord Almighty"

(Isa 6:5). God's revelation of himself to his servants is a dangerous gift. On the one hand, to touch the mountain of God is to touch mystery, danger, and possible death. "It is a terrible thing to fall into the hands of the living God" (Heb 10:31). There is danger in the coming of light. But on the other hand, when God draws near to his frail human creatures, he does so in order to share his light with them and to equip them with the faculty of spiritual sight. In the infinite space between divine revelation and human understanding lies the necessity for the people of faith to understand the mystery that surrounds them. In response to God's call on our lives, we live on the threshold of knowing and not knowing, obedience and disobedience. We are called to belong to a "kingdom of light" (Col 1:12) and to live out of the resources we find there. An excess of light also means that when we draw near to God we not only know him more fully, but we come to know ourselves more clearly. Amidst the miracle of theophany (the appearance of God), encounter, and self-revelation, God searches our hearts by his Spirit. The impulses, motives, and desires of the human heart are brought to the surface where we can come to know ourselves as God knows us, naked before the light.

The second warning concerning light from Christian spirituality is that of darkness. Because God dwells in unapproachable light and cannot be observed in his pure essence, it is commonplace for saints and mystics to employ two different kinds of language to refer to two different kinds of theology: the *kataphatic* and the *apophatic*. The kataphatic (meaning "affirmation through direct speech") suggests God can be known positively by reason and the human senses. Saints and mystics alike testify to the nearness of God who is closer than a brother and who is nearer than hands and feet. He is the object of our desire and the one who we love with the loving centers of our hearts. But God cannot be captured, domesticated, or limited to our small understandings. The idea of the apophatic (meaning "negation" or "through indirect speech") refers to the void in our understanding of God. The void arises because God is ineffable and beyond the capacity of our mortal minds to grasp. That is, the eternal cannot be circumscribed or encompassed. Yet even in the darkness, and even in our finitude, God's plenitude shines upon us. Negative theology is a way of saying that God is God and we are not. It is a way of admitting that the darkness that encompasses us should not cause us to cease our quest for God. The darkness arises because there is too much light, such that we cannot see him. Think of looking into the sun and you will understand the concept of apophatic theology. There is so much light that we must look away. The brightness is too much for us to bear. We know the sun is there because we can feel its heat surrounding and embracing us, yet we cannot look into the sun or see its rays. A theology of darkness arises when we focus too much on the eye of faith. There are times when we must sit in the midst of mystery, wonder, and awe, trusting those senses within us that tell us through participatory knowing that God is near, that God is within us, and that God is for us.

Yet the Christian understanding of light is that Jesus is the one who most truly reveals the Father. Jesus is the "true light that gives light to every man" (John 1:9), and the one who came to do the works of him who sent him to reveal the Father to his followers. Because of Jesus, we are no longer in the dark concerning God's identity or motives. Because God has "made his light shine in our hearts to give us the light of the knowledge of the glory of God in the face of Christ" (2 Cor 4:6), Christians have a theology of light that identifies Christ as its source, and the One who came to give his people the gift of spiritual vision. In Christ, in his life, his face, his works, his death and resurrection, his salvation—we can see into the very heart and mind of God. This is why the Apostle Paul can say that the spiritually enlivened and awakened soul has access to the "mind of Christ" (1 Cor 2:16), wherein lies the very "thoughts of God" (2:11).

CHRISTIAN ENLIGHTENMENT

The notion of enlightenment is well-known among students of world religions as something belonging to Buddhism. It has achieved what I would call the status of general knowledge in the minds of most people around the world. Buddhist enlightenment begins in the sixth-century BC, in the experience of the young Indian prince Gautama Buddha. Heavily protected by his parents inside the cloister of the family palace, Gautama was completely unaware of the limit conditions that bedevil human existence. But he escaped the palace and saw for the first time the four passing sights of a decrepit old man (mortality), a sick man (suffering), a dead man (death), and a monk (humanity's religious quest). In response to these sights he renounced his royal heritage, stripped off his fine clothes, and began the search for salvation. Finally, at the age of thirty-five and after a long search, he sat beneath the bo tree in search of wisdom and enlightenment. According to Buddhist tradition he sat there for forty-nine days, overcoming his confusion of mind and the temptations which assailed him, to emerge from his deep contemplation as The Enlightened One. Buddha's quest for wisdom and truth revealed the Four Noble Truths and the Noble Eightfold Path. Today these teachings inform the substance and practice of the world's more than seven hundred million Buddhists.

Not so well-known, however, is the spiritual enlightenment that belongs to Christianity. Indeed, a long and continuous history of enlightenment has been maintained within the Judeo-Christian tradition. It commences in the biblical record, is picked up and developed by such writers as St. Augustine, the church fathers, Bonaventure, and Ignatius, and enlightenment continues to be an underlying theme in the contemporary Christian spiritual experience for believers all around the world. Christian enlightenment is the bestowal of a Christ-centered spiritual insight onto those individuals and communities who express their faith in Christ and who consciously participate in the life of the Spirit. *Enlightenment* is a biblical word. The apostle Paul prayed that the "eyes of your hearts may be enlightened in order that you may know the hope to which he (Christ) has called you, the riches of his glorious inheritance in the saints" (Eph 1:18).[1] The writer to the Hebrews spoke of enlightenment in the past tense, when he warned the early Christians not to backslide and fall away. "It is impossible for those who have once been enlightened, who have tasted the heavenly gift, who have shared in the Holy Spirit, who have tasted the goodness of the word of God in the powers of the coming age, if they fall away, to be brought back to repentance, because to their loss they are crucifying the Son of God all over again and subjecting him to public disgrace (Heb 6:4–6)."

The writer to the Hebrews adopted the past tense because he knew that everyone who had met Christ for themselves had been changed in some fundamental way. They looked at the world differently, they thought differently, they had been taken to new places and shown things that did not belong to them, and so the idea of giving up their transformative experience in order to go back to their old "blindness" was a travesty. The Apostle Paul prayed that the Ephesian Christians would

---

1. The Greek stem is *photismos*, from which we get our *photo*graph or *photo*synthesis. The passive mood is used here indicating that someone other than the human subject does the "enlightening" of the eyes, namely Christ.

have the eyes of their hearts opened so they would know things directly related to the themes of hope, inheritance, and power. Enlightenment is not something we have to sneak into Christianity through the back door; it is a concept that belongs natively to it. Christ—the truly Enlightened One "in whom are hidden all the treasures of wisdom and knowledge" (Col 2:3)—awakens, enlightens, and enlivens his followers and delivers them into a new place via a new way of knowing and being.

The Buddhist and the Christian understandings of enlightenment differ in three significant ways. First, in extent. Buddhist enlightenment is limited. It is given only to those few spiritual elites (or bodhisattvas) who qualify for nirvana, and who delay their departure for the next life or the next level in order to serve the needs of a common humanity. By contrast, Christian enlightenment is given to everyone who undergoes conversion or what Jesus called the "new birth" (John 3:3). The new birth is the most basic transformation of the Christian faith. Christian enlightenment is the experience of being illumined, which follows from turning to Christ, and is the standard-issue experience of salvation for all followers of Christ. At the center of the Christian faith experience is regeneration, which is available to all believers through a transformation of their consciousness.

The second difference between the Buddhist and Christian understanding of enlightenment is its source. Buddhist enlightenment is the outcome of an enlarged consciousness that arises inside the person who exercises the Eightfold Noble Path and practices right views, right resolve, right speech, right conduct, right livelihood, right effort, right attention, and right meditation. In other words, the source of Buddhist enlightenment arises in the human person who by his or her own efforts obtains insight into the cosmic consciousness. In Christian enlightenment, the source of the awakening is Christ himself. As the one who is the light of the world, Christ bestows his light upon his followers. That light takes up residence in the human heart and becomes the guiding light for Christian disciples. It occurs when the believing soul has something like scales "fall from their eyes"—as the Apostle Paul experienced at his conversion (Acts 9:18). Believers experience a lifting of the "veil . . . from their minds" (2 Cor 3:14–18). Christian believers are "made new in the attitude of their minds" (Eph 4:23) by being "renewed in knowledge in the image of [their] Creator" (Col 3:10).

And the third difference is in result. Buddhist enlightenment for most practitioners is a distant future anticipation. It remains an unlikely expectation; they do not receive it in this life. Their lives are bent toward qualifying for enlightenment through participation in Buddhist practices. But Christian enlightenment, on the contrary, is a present reality that informs and shapes the Christian's mode of seeing and knowing (epistemology), as well as the basis on which they see and know (ontology). The result of enlightenment in the life of Christian believers is that they understand themselves to exist in the presence of God. Their experience of being enlightened is not a qualifying essay, but the fruit of a Godward life. Believers can live now in the same jubilant mode as they expect to live their future lives in the presence of God, when heaven has come to earth. Christian enlightenment is not a wistful longing for, but an energetic participation in the life of God.

A LITURGY OF LIGHT

Theologically, the cross lies at the center of Christian belief. And experientially, Christians have placed the cross at the center of their discipleship. Christianity is, after all, the crucified church following in the footsteps of its crucified Messiah. Jesus not only called his disciples to "Come, follow me," but he also called them to take up their cross daily: "for whoever wants to save his life will lose it, but whoever loses his life for me will save it" (Luke 9:23–24). Without doubt, Christianity is cruciform. To demonstrate the point, one of the central features of Christian worship is the Stations of the Cross with its Via Dolorosa ("pathway of suffering"). The traditional Stations of the Cross are:[2]

Station 1: Pilate condemns Jesus to death (Luke 23:20–25; Mark 15:1–15).

Station 2: Jesus receives the cross (John 19:17; Mark 15:20).

Station 3: Jesus falls to the ground for the first time.

Station 4: Jesus meets his mother.

Station 5: Simon of Cyrene is obliged to carry the cross (Mark 15:21; Luke 23:36).

---

2. Ford-Grabowsky, *Stations of the Light*, 22–23.

Station 6: Veronica wipes Jesus' face.

Station 7: Jesus falls a second time.

Station 8: Jesus talks to the women of Jerusalem (Luke 23:27–31).

Station 9: Jesus falls a third time.

Station 10: Jesus is stripped of his garments.

Station 11: Jesus is nailed to the cross (Mark 15:22–26; Luke 23:32–34).

Station 12: Jesus dies on the cross (Matt 27:45–50; Mark 15:33–37).

Station 13: Jesus' body is taken down from the cross.

Station 14: Jesus' body is placed in the tomb (Matt 27:57–61; Mark 15:46).

The Stations of the Cross are intended to help worshippers participate in Jesus' suffering as he makes his journey to the cross to redeem a lost and reprobate humanity.

But the cross is not all there is to spirituality in the Jesus tradition. Christianity does not end with the cross; it begins with the cross. Beyond the cross, beyond suffering, and beyond death are Jesus' resurrection, ascension, and rule. Beyond the tears, the tyranny, and the terror of Jesus' crucifixion are his joy, his laughter, and the light of his kingdom. Lest Christians always be consigned to a painful spirituality, they are invited to participate in a liturgy that follows on from the Stations of the Cross to a joyful spirituality that enables them to share in a liturgy of light. As Ford-Grabowsky records them, the Stations of the Light, or the Via Lucis, are:[3]

Station 1: Jesus rises from the dead (Matt 28:5–6).

Station 2: The women find the empty tomb (Matt 28:1–6).

Station 3: The risen Lord appears to Mary Magdalene (John 20:16).

Station 4: Mary Magdalene proclaims the resurrection to the apostles (John 20:18).

Station 5: The risen Lord appears on the Road to Emmaus (Luke 24:13–27).

---

3. Ford-Grabowsky, *Stations of the Light*, 4.

Station 6: The risen Lord is recognised in the breaking of the bread (Luke 24:28–32).

Station 7 The risen Lord appears to the disciples in Jerusalem (Luke 24:36–39).

Station 8: The risen Lord gives the disciples the power to forgive (John 20:22–23a).

Station 9: The risen Lord strengthens the faith of Thomas (John 20:24–29).

Station 10: The risen Lord says to Peter, "Feed my sheep" (John 21:15–17).

Station 11: The risen Lord sends his disciples into the world (Matt 28:16–20).

Station 12: The risen Lord ascends into heaven (Acts 1:9–11).

Station 13: Apostles and others wait with Mary in the Upper Room (Acts 1:12–14).

Station 14: The risen Lord sends the Holy Spirit (Acts 2:2–4).

The Stations of Light enable Christian worshippers to participate in a joyful liturgy in which Jesus transitions from the man of sorrows on the cross to the glorious Lord of history seated on his regal throne. The Stations of the Light also enables worshippers to transition their experience of anguish, sorrow, struggle, and despair to the joy, delight, and ecstasy that belong to them in Christ. The movement is one from suffering to celebration; and from chalice to crown. Historically, Jesus' disciples have always understood the need to transition beyond the cross to resurrection. Theologically, Jesus' disciples have always confessed the reality of heaven in the midst of the material world. And experientially, Jesus' disciples have always practiced their redemption in a fallen world. Christians are a joyful people whose lives are lived here on earth out of the resources of heaven. Christianity is not a half-finished faith that produces half-finished people. Instead, it is a finished faith whose story and whose energy is intended to grow ordinary people into extraordinary people who become giants of character, giants of hope, giants of joy. Overwhelming joy and delight ought to be the predominating spirit of the true Christian, rather than a predisposition towards an unhealthy self-hatred and repressive guilt. Why? Because Christ—the bringer of light—has liberated his people from darkness and has invited them to become little christs among the ruins and ashes of the communities and life circumstances where they live and move and have their being.

But when Jesus says, "*I* am the light of the world" (John 8:12), that is not the end of it. For he also says to his disciples, "*You* are the light of the world" (Matt 5:14). In giving his disciples this elevated title, Jesus did not wish to indicate that Christians are small-s saviors or that the light originated with them. On the contrary, he is suggesting that Christian disciples of every kind, place, and time have a part to play and a share in his task of disseminating light into a world that is otherwise dark and gloomy. Christianity is a way of light!

CITIZENS OF TWO WORLDS

We are told that "the disciples were first called Christians in Antioch" (Acts 11:26). There is some suggestion that the name "Christian," while it was eventually adopted by the believers, may initially have been an unfriendly nickname coined by their opponents.[4] The term *Christian* (meaning "Christ's ones") has now become widely recognized among Jesus' followers around the world, but there was a time when it sat uncomfortably between *Chrestus* (meaning "good" or "goodie-two-shoes") and *cretin* (meaning "retarded" or "numbskull"). What did the Christians call themselves? There are many word usages employed in the New Testament, such as, followers, saints, believers, the brethren, or "followers of the Way." But there seems to be one special word that believers applied to themselves; namely *paroikoi*, meaning "aliens," "temporary residents," "strangers on the earth," or "citizens of God's world" (Acts 7:6; 87:29; Eph 2:19; and 1 Pet 2:11).

It is this latter usage that the authors Hauerwas and Willimon adopt in their book, *Resident Aliens*.[5] The book is a brilliant take on the challenges that face Christian believers in juggling their existence between two worlds—this earthly world and the heavenly world of which they are dual citizens. Right in the center of the book is the nub of what the authors want to say. Like the well-known statement, "You are what you

---

4. See for example, Kreider, *Worship and Evangelism*, 1995.
5. Hauerwas and Willimon, *Resident Aliens*, 1991.

eat," Hauerwas and Willimon tell us "we are what we see."[6] We can only act on what we can see and know is there. The Christian vision that arises out of the "stunning vision of reality [Christians] see in the life, death, and resurrection of Jesus" is radically different to the authorized version of right-mindedness that pertains in the everyday world.[7] As followers of Jesus Christ, Christians are citizens of the kingdom of God.[8] And from that vantage point Christians have a particular way of looking at the world which is christocentric.

Jesus did not leave a book, a building, a school, or even a religion. Instead, he left a people. And into that people (think back to Muggeridge's idea of the "third testament") he embedded the substance of the kingdom he came to establish. In just the same way that the stained-glass image of Jesus at the front of my childhood church was a pictorialized form of the gospel, so the church is an embodied and enfleshed form of the gospel in 3-D form. The missionary statesman Lesslie Newbigin made the insightful statement: "The only answer, the only hermeneutic of the gospel, is a congregation of men and women who believe it [the gospel] and live by it."[9]

In September 2006 I had a conversation with Michael Horsburgh, a long-time professor of social work in a Sydney university.[10] We were talking about how people know things. Michael's contribution to the conversation was one I have not forgotten. He made the statement, "In social work it is commonly accepted that the entire technology of the discipline is embodied in the person of the social worker, who carries within themselves all the tools and techniques they need to convey their craft." This statement was, he told me,—the fruit of thirty years of teaching social work in the classroom. It is a startling statement because it powerfully captures what I am trying to convey to you about discipleship. The entire know-how of discipleship is embodied in the person of the believer who carries within themselves all the knowledge and apparatus he or she needs to express their calling as a follower of Christ.

Christians have "the kingdom of God within [them]" (Luke 17:21). They are a revolutionary people who have a Christ-given capacity to

6. Ibid., 83.
7. Ibid., 75.
8. Phil 3:20; "But our citizenship is in heaven."
9. Newbigin. *Gospel in a Pluralist Society*, 227.
10. With permission.

carry the Christ light within them and to effect a powerful change in the society around them. That change is not based on rational or moral argument, but is based on the compelling and transformed lives they lead. That change is also made on the basis that the light of Christ within them is visible to all who observe the embodied gospel at work inside them.

The end result of God's people who truly fulfill their calling within eye shot of those who do not yet believe is what Esther Meek called "epistemological therapy."[11] Epistemological therapy is when a false view of the world is replaced with a correct view, thus ensuring that the Christian point of view is not only heard but seen, and seen to be a valid and authentic counterpoint to the authorized version of right-mindedness that applies in the world. It does however require that the church overcome its false gospels and its narrow-minded sectarianism and be willing to take the plank out of its own eye before it begins to offer any form of therapy to non-Christian outsiders (Matt 7:5).

Returning to Hauerwas and Willimon's notion of Christians as resident aliens, it can be said that in the midst of our current world, which can be described as a culture of desire, the politics of violence, and the loss of any sense of purpose or direction, Christians offer a counter-point alternative characterized by right living, right being, and right thinking. Instead of being trapped in the bland cul-de-sac of shopping-mall consumerism, Christians set out on an adventure to discover a radical freedom and a purposeful existence that is the gift of God to humanity:

> [The church's] biblical story demands an offensive rather than a defensive posture . . . The world and all its resources, anguish, gifts, and groaning is God's world, and God demands what God has created. Jesus Christ is the supreme act of divine intrusion into the world's settled arrangements. In Christ, God refuses to "stay in his place." The message that sustains the colony [of resident aliens] is not for itself but for the whole world—the colony having significance only as God's means for saving the whole world. The colony is God's means of a major offensive against the world, for the world.[12]

The church is God's gift to the world. We have a story to tell. We have a vision of reality to share that is different from any other story. Ours is a call to participate in a divinely originated counter reality. "In

---

11. Meek, *Loving to Know*, 3–30.
12. Hauerwas and Willimon, *Resident Aliens*, 51.

Jesus, we meet not a representation of basic ideas about God, world and humanity, but an invitation to join up, to become part of the movement, a people."[13] The church is the colony of God's habitation on earth. But before we try to convince the unbelieving world of the need to believe in Christ, the church has to know what it believes, knows, and sees. We need to get our own story straight first if we are to fulfil our mission of presenting the gospel of light to a people in great darkness.

CONCLUSION

In this chapter we have discovered that Jesus invited his followers to become citizens of his kingdom, which is a kingdom of light. *Christianity is a way of light.* As Michael Casey says, "Beyond our mundane experience lies another world. When the door opens and we pass into it, the meaning of our life changes, and we experience everything against a different horizon."[14] So, from Jesus to Paul, from Paul to the churches in Asia, from the Christianized philosophy of Alexandria to Athanasius the theologian of light, to the Eastern Orthodox Churches whose theology continues to speak of the church as an illumined community who follow Christ the Giver of Light, to the Roman Catholic Church that has offered us the Liturgy of Light, to Evangelical churches that preach the light of Christ to "open their eyes and turn them from darkness to light" (Acts 26:18), to Holiness churches that focus on being moral agents who have "nothing to do with darkness" (2 Cor 6:14), to Pentecostal churches that desire to see heaven opened—Christianity is a way of light. It is a kingdom of light where, in the light of Christ, we are both enlightened and made capable of seeing light for what it truly is. "In your light we see light" (Ps 36:9).

> *Into the Light*
> God is wider than the galaxies
> And underneath my skin
> He's out there in the universe
> And present deep within
> He is there in every atom
> And wider than the sky

13. Ibid., 21.
14. Casey, *Fully Human Fully Divine*, 202.

I cannot get away from God
And I'm not going to try
I have seen His Spirit shining
From a hundred midnight skies
I have felt his Spirit speaking
To that space behind my eyes
He can speak to me in thunder
Or that quiet inner voice
And my ego melts to nothing
For I know I have no choice
But to willingly go with him
And to let his purpose be
For nothing I could do myself
Could mean as much to me
God witnessed my conception
He knew me at my birth
For the God who lives in heaven
Is the God who came to earth
He controls the claps of thunder
And the rolling of the sea
Yet the God who holds the planets
Is the God who lives in me.
Call it my conversion
You can call it second birth
You can say we get to heaven
By the choices made on earth
Call it my baptism
You can call it what you like
But I stepped out of darkness
When I stepped into the light.[15]

---

15. Haddon, Sydney, July 2007. Used with permission.

6

The Way of Wisdom

"Those who are spiritual discern all things" (1 Cor 2:15 NRSV).

IN THIS CHAPTER WE will explore the Christian spiritual pathway as a way of wisdom. Jesus' disciples—in first-century Palestine and in twenty-first-century Vancouver (or wherever you live)—are invited to sit at Jesus' feet and to "Learn from [him]" (Matt 11:29). Wisdom, insight, and discernment are central features of the Christian spiritual pathway. But what does it mean for Christian disciples to discern all things and to have a share in the "mind of Christ" (1 Cor 2:16)?

MERE CHRISTIANS

In the 1960s, the zoo in Perth, Western Australia, had an exhibit they neither could nor, I'm certain, would have today. They had a chimpanzee named Jimmy who smoked cigarettes. Visitors to the zoo could observe Jimmy's cast iron cage, located between the main entrance gate and the refreshments kiosk. Many people offered him food and cigarettes, which he accepted. He crouched or stood on his hind legs, leaning against the frame of the cage smoking his cigarette. He looked for all the world, like, well, like an everyday human person. People who own pets often comment on the humanlike qualities of their animals' facial expressions, moods, and at times even their intelligence. Jimmy seemed to be "one of us" as he smoked, looking out on the world while thinking perhaps about the weather, or his long lost love, or what he might prepare for dinner. Of course Jimmy was not a human being, he was a chimpanzee. But many who watched him acting like a human thought of him as such because he seemed to participate in a human world.

In this chapter I want us to think about human believers who, despite their limitations, claim to participate in God's world, God's life, and God's purposes. They claim to draw near to God in worship. They claim to speak to God in prayer. They claim to have in their possession written correspondence from God. They claim to share table fellowship with God. And they claim to have a love relationship with God. Please understand that I'm not suggesting that Christians are chimpanzees. What I am engaging with here is the remarkable capacity for human beings (lower-order creatures) to have an affinity and relationship with God (a higher-order being). Readers will of course have a range of opinions about Jimmy the chimpanzee: maybe he was just an animal who spent so much time among humans that he began to act like them. Or maybe Jimmy was more human than we might be prepared to think. Whatever we might say about Jimmy and his degree of humanness, Christians would say of themselves that, because they have been created in the image of God and because they have been uniquely fitted for a relationship with God, people who confess faith in God begin to act like him, look like him, and even think like him. They come to adopt a God's-eye point of view and to espouse in their beliefs and teachings the kinds of wisdom that are more likely to be found in the mind of God than in the minds of humans.

The remarkable thing is just how unlikely this is. That mere mortals could have access to the wisdom that belongs to God is all but unthinkable. Yet that is what the Apostle Paul suggested when he wrote to the Corinthian Christians saying, "not many of you were wise by human standards; not many were influential; not many were of noble birth . . . but we have the mind of Christ" (1 Cor 1:26; 2:16). God, it seems, has a policy of bringing rough and smooth together, humanity and divinity together, not knowing and knowing together, and jars of clay and treasure together. He has deliberately chosen a strategy of selecting the odds and ends of society to become his elect people in order to prove a point. And the point is that God's wisdom makes more sense than human wisdom. What people from outside the faith who adhere to the authorized version of right-mindedness call "foolishness" is in fact a specially minted form of wisdom that belongs to God. And God is interested in sharing that wisdom with those who belong to him.

In the second century AD, Celsus, a Roman critic of Christianity, sneered at the kinds of uneducated and lower-class people the Christian communities gathered to themselves. He described the way ordinary Christians shared their knowledge of Christ whenever and wherever they could:

> In private houses we see wool workers, cobblers, laundry workers, and the most illiterate and bucolic yokels ["rough, outback"], who would not dare say anything at all to their elders and more intelligent masters. But whenever they get hold of children in private and some stupid women with them, they let out some astounding statements such as, for example, that they must not pay any attention to their fathers and school teachers, but must obey *them*; they say that these talk nonsense and have no understanding, and that in reality neither know nor are able to do anything good, and are taken up with mere empty chatter. But they alone, they say, know the right way to live, and if the children would believe them, they would become happy and make their home happy as well.[1]

Cardinal John Henry Newman extended this unflattering description of the early Christians, using the words of their earliest critics, suggesting that Christians turned away the educated and cultured in favor of the crass, illiterate, and ignorant among the population.[2] He describes how the servant class and tradesmen left their hammers and washing baskets to preach about the things of heaven. Even the church fathers themselves confirmed the insignificance of their fellow believers. Cardinal Newman has provided a suite of such descriptions in the words of leading individuals from the early church. Athenagoras spoke of the virtue of the "ignorant men, mechanics, and old women." "They are gathered," says St. Jerome, "not from the Academy or Lyceum, but from the low populace." "They are whitesmiths, servants, farm laborers, woodmen, men of sordid trades, beggars," says Theodoret. "We are engaged in the farm, in the market, at the baths, wine shops, stables, and fairs; as seamen, as soldiers, as peasants, as dealers," says Tertullian.[3]

How did such men and women come to be converted? And once converted, how did these unpolished people come to assert that the wisdom and knowledge they possessed exceeded and surpassed the highest wisdom the classical Greco-Roman world had to offer? These men and

---

1. Wilkins, *Christians as the Romans Saw Them*, 97.
2. Newman, *Grammar of Ascent*, 361–62.
3. Ibid.

women were illiterate and unlettered; they were without the benefit of the educational training enjoyed by their employers, yet they presumed to venture forth to teach and induct others into their unique form of knowledge.

It is obvious that these unschooled and unlettered men and women found themselves in possession of a form of wisdom and insight that did not originate with them. As a result of their encounter with Christ, their reading the Scriptures, their associating with the faith community who worshipped Jesus as the Lord of history, they had come to indwell a biblically formed world that revolved around a sin-salvation-sanctification hermeneutic. They were divine nobodies who had been delivered into the supernatural and transformative world of Christian spiritual knowing. It was these unlettered men and women who laid the foundation for the revolution that brought about the conversion of the known world to Christ and who changed the minds of the intelligentsia of their day. Like the disciples before them, they amazed their opponents because the only form of wisdom they possessed arose out of the fact that "they had been with Jesus" (Acts 4:13).

Two key words can be used to describe the kinds of transformation of consciousness that occurs when someone comes to believe in Christ. The first word is *God-taught*. The Apostle Paul created a one-off word for the experience of being taught by God (*theodidaktos* in 1 Thess 4:9).[4] In the single instance in which it is used, *theodidaktos* does not refer to a series of intellectual propositions but to the quality of interpersonal relationships expressed among the community of believers. This idea is strongly linked to Jesus' words, "they will know you are my disciples by your love for one another" (John 13:35). Perhaps this is intended to reflect the quality of interpersonal relations within the godhead. It is certainly an example of the participatory knowledge we spoke of previously, which is characterized by whole-person knowing, and which often expresses itself through interpersonal relationships. This form of interpersonal wholeness is a sign of the presence of the kingdom of God in their midst.

The second word that describes the kind of transformed consciousness that occurs at conversion when someone comes to believe in Christ is *transvaluation*. The Catholic philosopher Bernard Lonergan described

---

4. *Theodidaktos* is a composite word, from *theo* meaning "God" and *didaktos* meaning "to teach or be taught" in First Thessalonians 4:9.

the results of conversion as the "transvaluation of value," seeking to identify the extent of the religious change that has occurred in what one knows and sees and how one knows and sees—as a result of the radical shift in peoples' consciousness.[5] That shift in consciousness moves from an earthly to a heavenly reference point, from a natural to a supernatural reference point, and from a human to a divine reference point. Everything they previously knew or thought to be true has now been repositioned, allowing them to live life on a higher plane of existence. No wonder the early Christians turned the world upside down. They had become divine nobodies who had been grasped by life itself, who had begun to live out of the wisdom and resources of God himself.

THOSE WHO ARE SPIRITUAL

In his first letter to the church at Corinth, the Apostle Paul contrasts the modes of understanding and knowing experienced by the unbeliever and the believer. The passage is 1 Cor 1:18—2:16.[6] Let's look at the passage in more detail.

1. 1 Corinthians 1:18–25. God's wisdom is contrasted with human wisdom: Corinth was a very cosmopolitan city that became the capital of Roman-controlled Greece. It was an important center for politics, sport, learning, and religion (the major landmark was the temple of Apollo). It is likely that the newly established Christian congregation in Corinth felt threatened in its surroundings and needed reassurance by the apostle that their faith was no less wise or relevant than those teachings found in the Jewish synagogues or the Greek places of learning. Paul wrote that contrary to human expectation, it is not the educated person or the scholar who has true wisdom, but the Christian believer.

2. 1 Corinthians1:26–31. The "foolish" Christian community: The Christian community included many among its number from the lower classes—especially women, children, and slaves. They had little,

---

5. Lonergan, Bernard. "Lonergan Responds," 227.

6. The translators of the NIV Bible adopted the gender-specific word *man*. They have done so in keeping with the text of the Greek New Testament, which makes use of masculine pronouns and suffixes. I have adjusted the language to be more gender representative to read "spiritual person" instead of "spiritual man."

if any, opportunity to be educated and because of their social status would not have been given any recognition by the wider society. They knew that by the standards of the prevailing culture they were not influential and were unlikely to be taken seriously by the citizens of Corinth. Yet it is precisely to these low-born people that God revealed himself so as to shame the wise people of this world.

3. 1 Corinthians 2:1–5. Paul's weak preaching: By his own admission, Paul's preaching was not eloquent and was not carried out in the self-styled superior wisdom typical of the rhetoric of his day (although it seems he was trained in rhetoric). He approached his task in weakness and fear, but he was accompanied by the Spirit's power so that the faith of the Corinthian Christians did not rest on men's wisdom but on God's wisdom. Paul's discussion of power evoked a knowledge contest between the gods, through which God demonstrated his supreme wisdom in the redemptive purpose that Jesus came to accomplish. God's wisdom was to be proved and demonstrated in the lives of ordinary people—these "mere" Christians.

4. 1 Corinthians 2:6–10a. God's wisdom revealed: The content of Paul's preaching, communicated in humility, was a secret wisdom that had long been hidden but has now been made known in Christ. Paul's proclamation of salvation through faith in Christ appealed to the kind of existence people might have wished was available to them, and dreamt might exist, but could find no way to access. It was this kind of existence that God had called into being—commanded, prepared, implemented—and now made available to those men and women who were prepared to imagine it and to receive it through faith in Christ.

5. 1 Corinthians 2:10b–12. The Spirit reveals God's wisdom: Paul uses the rhetorical device of arguing from the lesser to the greater, appealing to his readers' innate knowledge of their own inner thoughts and psychological functioning. Just as a human person knows their own thoughts because their inner spirit reveals it to them, so the Spirit of God knows the deepest innermost thoughts of God and makes them known to the disciples so that they may understand what God has given them in Christ.

6. 1 Corinthians 2:13–16. The unspiritual and the spiritual person: Paul continues to compare the two forms of knowledge by representing

them in personal form, first in the nonbeliever and second in the Christian believer. To the unspiritual person (Greek, *psukikos*, meaning "natural" and "guided by human reason alone"), God's words and ways make no sense because they can only be discerned (Greek, *krino*, meaning "examined" or "judged") with the help of the Spirit who is absent in his life. But the spiritual person (Greek, *pneumatikos*, "guided by the Spirit") is able to understand all that he encounters in the physical and the spiritual domains because the Spirit of God has shown it to him so that he may understand what God has given to him in Christ (cf. v.12). While the spiritual person may be subject to the unspiritual person in matters of politics and economics, this is not the case when it comes to making judgments in the spiritual realm. Indeed, the unspiritual person must submit to what the spiritual person knows concerning the wisdom of God. At the end of Paul's chapter comes the stunning disclosure that the spiritual person has access to God's thought processes to the extent that the spiritual person "has the mind of Christ" (v.16b).

Possessing the mind of Christ is a concept that needs to be carefully understood. It does not mean a brain transplant, to know everything God knows, or the capacity to think God's actual concrete thoughts. Nor does it mean that we share in God's attributes of omnipotence, omniscience, and omnipresence, or that we have direct access to everything that God thinks. Nor does it mean to be possessed by God's thoughts in a way that displaces human thinking or freedom. That goes too far. The psalmist rightly admits that "Such knowledge is too wonderful for me, too lofty for me to attain" (Ps 139:6). There is no room for pride, egotism, or mistaken thinking here.

Rather, having access to the mind of Christ means that the believing soul has access to some of the key indicators of how and what God thinks. Christians understand that their knowledge of God is tempered by their mortality and the opaqueness of the glass of vision through which they see. What knowledge the Christian does have of God is only what is graciously given them by God himself, therefore all Christian knowledge is in a very real way mediated knowledge. "*Now* I know in part; [but] *then* I shall know fully, even as I am fully known" (13:12b).

Nevertheless there is within the Christian believing soul a deposit of faith that enables them to know with certainty that God has spoken to them. Between the scripturally fashioned awareness—the presence of the Spirit of God within them, the faith of the believing community that has been taught to them, and the perceptive eye of faith that alerts them to the presence of God at work in their lives.

Paul's letter to the Corinthian church allows us to better understand those spiritual dynamics that enable a person to either see or not see spiritually, and how it is that the spiritual person sees into the spiritual realm to know and understand its substance. This is the goal of Jesus' mission to eyes and ears.

CHRIST THE WISDOM OF GOD

Wisdom is central to the human quest for self-understanding. This concept applies as much to citizens of the ancient world as it does to those of us who live in the contemporary postmodern world. Much of the history of the ancient world is bent on seeking out wisdom that could explain the mystery that surrounds our human existence. Thomas Hobbes described human life as "solitary, poor, nasty, brutish and short."[7] Where then "can wisdom be found? Where does understanding dwell?" (Job 28:12).

In one sense, Greek philosophy, the advice of the Oracle at Delphi to "Know thyself!", the tragedies, and the best poetry and literature throughout history have all tried to answer this same set of basic questions: "Who am I?" "Where am I?" "What's wrong?" and "What is the remedy?"[8] These questions often involve us asking a set of parallel questions about God i.e., "Who is God?" "What resources lie in its, his, or her being?" "Is it possible to live a God-pleasing life?", and "Where do I find the wisdom I need to make sense of my life?"

Wisdom (Hebrew, *hokma*, meaning "knowledge" or "insight") is not just a vague concept in the Old Testament. It is a specific category of knowledge represented by an entire genre or body of work. The Wisdom literature in the Old Testament is represented by such books as Job, Ecclesiastes, Psalms, Proverbs, Lamentations, the Song of Solomon, and numerous passages from the prophetic literature. In ancient Israel, wisdom was thought to be an attribute of God himself, for it is God who "gives wisdom to the wise and knowledge to the discerning" (Dan 2:21). Wisdom

---

7. Hobbes, *Leviathan*, 78.
8. Walsh and Middleton, *Transforming Vision*, 35.

begins with the "fear of the Lord" (Ps 111:10) and is reflected in the character and the dispositions of men and women who are close to God. Wisdom is more than a set of propositions. Instead, wisdom is a way of understanding and interpreting how things are in the world. *Wisdom is a form of embodied moral knowledge, put in place by God as a type of manufacturer's instructions for life.* On paying due attention to the getting of wisdom, these instructions become embedded in the lives of the people of God. Education that has true wisdom at its heart is concerned as much with the learner's values and capacity to make careful judgments as it is with facts and figures. As such, the primary concern of Wisdom literature is to invite the reader to discover the truthfulness of its teachings, and to instill and bequeath those insights to the rising generations.

King Solomon was famous for his wisdom. "God gave Solomon wisdom and very great insight" (1 Kgs 4:29). When he was confronted by two women who both claimed to be the mother of the same child, Solomon called for a sword and threatened to cut the child in two, giving half to each woman. Out of love and compassion for the child, the birth mother relented and asked that he be given to the other woman (1 Kgs 3:16–38). The whole of the Middle East knew of Solomon's wisdom, and the Queen of Sheba visited him to see its extent for herself.

Wisdom is also identified as present alongside God at creation, reminding us that creation was not only good but also wise. Wisdom is depicted in personal and in feminine form as it calls out in the streets and public squares to prevent moral failure and to rebuke those who had become wise in their own eyes. Wisdom is not the automatic possession of everyone; it must be sought for and acquired with great diligence and persistence. "Get wisdom, get understanding . . . Though it cost all you have, get understanding" (Prov 4:6–7). But it is the Lord who gives wisdom and "from his mouth come knowledge and understanding" (Prov 2:6). In the apocryphal *Wisdom of Solomon*, the following description is given of wisdom herself:

> For there is in her a spirit quick of understanding, holy, alone in kind, manifold, subtil, freely moving, clear in utterance, unpolluted, distinct, unharmed, loving what is good, keen, unhindered, beneficent, loving towards man, steadfast, sure, free from care, all-powerful, all-surveying, and penetrating through all spirits that are quick of understanding, pure, most subtil: for wisdom is more mobile than any emotion; yea, she pervadeth and penetrateth all things by her pureness. For she is a breath of the power of God and a clear effluence of the glory of the Almighty;

therefore can nothing defiled find entrance into her. For she is an effulgence from everlasting light, and an unspotted mirror of the working of God and an image of his goodness. And she being one hath power to do all things; and remaining in herself, reneweth all things: and from generation to generation passing into holy souls she maketh them friends of God and prophets.[9]

From the perspective of the Old Testament, "All human knowledge comes back to the question about commitment to God . . . One becomes competent and expert as far as the orders in life are concerned only if one begins from knowledge about God."[10]

The New Testament has much to say about wisdom. From its earliest beginnings the Christian faith has been a wisdom tradition that has mediated the knowledge of God through Christ to its followers from earliest times. The New Testament continues the theme of wisdom begun in the Old Testament, but now positions Jesus Christ as the one who completes and fulfils the Old Testament archetype of wisdom. When Jesus taught that "wisdom is proved right by her actions" (Luke 7:31–35), we see him functioning very much in the tradition of the Jewish sage, but one who replaces traditional knowledge with God's wisdom. While it is likely that some of what Jesus had to say has been said by others at other times, there is something in the person, words, acts, and particularly in the death and resurrection of Christ for the salvation of the world that is truly unique. The Apostle John in his Gospel identified Jesus as the Logos of Hellenistic philosophy when he stated, "In the beginning was the Word, and the Word was with God, and the Word was God" (John 1:1). Greek philosophy understood the Logos to be the founding principle on which creation rested. Thus John identified Jesus with the personified Wisdom that accompanied God in his founding task of creation. The earliest disciples understood Jesus to be the authoritative interpreter of God's person and will. From the Christian point of view, "something [someone] greater than Solomon is here" (Matt 12:42).

It is in the writings of the Apostle Paul that we find some of the most compelling statements about Jesus as the wisdom of God. To the church in Ephesus, Paul wrote that God had "lavished on us *all wisdom and understanding*, [making] known to us the mystery of his will . . . to bring all things in heaven and on earth together under one head,

---

9. *Wisdom of Solomon, Apocrypha*, 174.
10. von Rad, *Wisdom in Israel*, 67.

even Christ" (Eph 1:8–10). He prayed for the Ephesians, asking God that he would enable them to "grasp how wide and long and high and deep is the love of Christ, and to know this love that *surpasses knowledge*—that [they] may be filled to the measure of all the fullness of God" (Eph 3:18–19). Further, in his letter to the believers in Colossae, Paul again prayed, asking "God to fill [them] with the knowledge of his will through all spiritual *wisdom and understanding*" (Col 1:9). It was to be in Christ—the one who is the image of the invisible God—that God was to rule over the created order, "reconciling to himself all things, whether things on earth or things in heaven, by making peace through his blood, shed on the cross" (Col 1:15, 20). Paul's purpose in writing was so that the Colossians would come to understand that they have "the full riches of complete understanding, in order that they may know the mystery of God, namely Christ, in whom are hidden *all the treasures of wisdom and knowledge*" (Col 2:2–3). Paul's readers needed to resist those forms of hollow and deceptive philosophy they encountered in the world (2:8), things which are only a shadow of those realities which are to be found in Christ (2:17), and so they will no longer be enemies with God in their minds (1:21). The result of "setting [their] minds on things above, not on earthly things" (3:2), was that they would "take off" their old selves, with their old practices and beliefs, and "put on" the new self, which has been "renewed in knowledge in the image of its Creator" (3:10). This is the type of the "spiritual man" referred to in 1 Corinthians 2 who participates in "the mind of Christ," which, in turn, produces the kind of transformative "renewing of your minds" Paul refers to in Romans 12:2.

From its very beginnings, the earliest Christian communities identified Christ as the originator of wisdom. Christians have always associated wisdom with Jesus, rather than in Greek philosophy, or the Jewish *Mishnah*, or the *Talmud*. A *sophos-Christology* developed very early in the Christian era, when Jesus was identified as personified Wisdom, and so became the cocreator with God and, who thus exceeded Solomon's wisdom. Wisdom (Greek, *sophia*, meaning "wisdom" or "instruction") in the Christian spiritual tradition begins and ends with Christ. To believe in Christ and set one's compass by his teaching is wisdom. But to reject his lordship and his cross is foolishness (Greek, *moria*, meaning "foolishness" or "senselessness").

There are three paradoxes at work here. First, Christian teaching has overthrown the established wisdom of the world, as exemplified by the exhortation to "Know thyself," and replaced it with the exhortation to "Know Christ!" To do this means coming to see eye-to-eye with Christ. This has been the persistent call of Christians in every time and place among their neighbors, friends, work colleagues, and family members. Second, Christian wisdom is not so much what you know as who you know (i.e., to know Jesus is to know and experience eternal life for oneself). A sophos-Christology is neither puerile doctrine nor a rational formula; rather, it is a form of interpersonal knowledge that has Christ at its center. And third, classical and religious forms of wisdom and knowledge are set aside in favor of something even more ancient and foundational, replacing natural wisdom with supernatural reality that arises out of Christ in whom are hidden "all the treasures of wisdom and knowledge" (Col 2:3).

THE TWO ENLIGHTENMENTS

In the final section of this chapter, I want to compare and contrast two enlightenments: first, the European humanist Enlightenment (ca. 1700–1800); and second, Christian spiritual enlightenment. During the European humanist Enlightenment, Immanuel Kant defined the Enlightenment in his *Religion within the Bounds of Reason Only* (1793) in the following way:

"The Enlightenment represents man's emergence from a self-inflicted state of [inferiority or] minority. A minor is one who is incapable of making use of his understanding without guidance from someone else . . . *Sapere aude*! (Enter wisdom!) Have the courage to make use of your own understanding, is therefore the watchword of the Enlightenment."[11]

The spirit of the Enlightenment was one of rationalism, scepticism, and self-sufficiency. No God, no priest, and no king were required to conduct one's affairs. All that was needed, it was thought, were the plain facts and a clear mind to locate solutions to any problem that confronted humanity. The grandchildren of the European Enlightenment are humanist education, scientific knowledge, and modern technology.

And second is the Christian spiritual enlightenment. In the previous chapter we contrasted the Buddhist understanding of enlighten-

---

11. Kant, in Detzler, "Enlightenment," 343–44.

ment and the Christian understanding of enlightenment, and described them as differing in extent, in source, and in result. Although, strangely, I have never heard a sermon or any teaching on the enlightenment that belongs to the Christian faith, there is such a thing as Christian spiritual enlightenment. It belongs natively to Christianity and deserves to be explored, for three simple reasons. First, enlightenment is a biblical word. The Apostle Paul prayed for the Ephesian Christians that the "eyes of their hearts may be enlightened" (Eph 1:18). Second, enlightenment has always been a primary element in Christian spiritual experience, arising from the transformed mind which is the normal state of the redeemed person. And third (and most convincingly), if Jesus is the bringer of light and the source of God's wisdom, submitting our lives to him results in us participating in a form of Christ-centered spiritual insight. Christians who follow Jesus the Sage become sagacious—not only in becoming as "wise as serpents and harmless as doves" (Matt 10:16)—but also in their willingness and ability to interpret the natural order through the lens of the Maker's instructions.

The question we are working our way towards answering in this section is twofold: (1) are the two enlightenments mutually exclusive and (2) to what extent should believers who have experienced Christian spiritual enlightenment take part in the first enlightenment, with particular reference to humanist education, scientific knowledge, and the high-tech technology that surrounds us as postmodern people? First, are the two enlightenments mutually exclusive? Atheists and secular thinkers would argue that they are exclusive; whereas most Christians I know would propose they are not. Without doubt the two enlightenments ask and answer different questions. The first enlightenment (the European Enlightenment) asks, "What are the physical laws that make the universe tick?" And the second enlightenment asks, "Why does the world exist and what is the purpose of human existence?" The Christian perspective on these two questions is that to answer the first question meaningfully obligates us to also answer the second question. As we indicated previously, all knowing is contextually bounded. For Christians the two enlightenments are not opposed to each other. The millions of Christian scientists, doctors, teachers, scholars, and intellectuals around the world are not being untrue to their faith when they use research and science to understand the biological world. Rather, they are "working out their salvation" by exerting their best efforts through research in order to understand the mysteries of the physical universe for the glory of God and the benefit of humanity. The foundations of modern science lie in exactly this place when the first scientists—many of whom held deep Christian convictions—determined that the best way to honor the Creator was to strive to understand his creation.

And second, to what extent should believers who have experienced Christian spiritual enlightenment take part in humanist education and scientific knowledge, and use the technology that surrounds us as the fruits of the European Enlightenment? It is true there are some people with Christian leanings who are deeply suspicious of the world and who want to abandon this world in favor of the safety of heaven. Such extreme world-denying groups and individuals are deeply uncomfortable being in the world. But the first task of the Christian disciple is not to escape the world by opting for the comfort of heaven. The first task of the Christian disciple is to bring heaven to earth. That is the whole point of the early Christian idea of *paroikoi*, where Christians were to set up colonies of heaven on earth to subvert the authorized version of right-mindedness by replacing it with a Christ-centered wisdom and way of life. This is not about religion, and it is not about politics—it is about being pro–*humanitas*; the gospel is good for humanity. So if you want my advice on these matters, get the best education you can, marshal as much intellectual muscle as you can muster, access the best technology you can, and "make your mark."[12]

Christians are not troglodytes. We simply answer the fundamental questions of existence in the proper order. *Who* and *why* questions deserve to be answered before *what* and *how* questions. We do this because we see life from the perspective of *sub specie aeternitatis* ("from the perspective of eternity").

For the Christian saint, all knowledge—including the knowledge of God—is defective and deficient unless and until it is knowledge of God through Christ. This is the testimony of Paul in his reinterpretation of the sophistry of the Hellenistic Judaism from earlier history, and it has been the testimony of Christians ever since. Unless it is properly grounded in the person of Jesus Christ who is the wisdom of God, in whom dwells the "full riches of complete understanding" of the mystery of God in

---

12. "Make your mark" is the motto of the Salvation Army in the Australian Eastern Territory, as they call for people to commit themselves to a life of service and commitment as Salvation Army soldiers and officers.

Christ (Col 2:2), it remains nothing more than human information that provides no useful input about the mysteries of either the natural or the supernatural orders. From where Christians stand, not to know Jesus as the Christ is to be adrift in a sea of relativism and at the mercy of a whole range of false gospels (i.e., consumerism, hedonism, gnosticism, philosophy, false religions, and no religion). Such a life is no life at all. It is to be "without hope and without God in the world" (Eph 2:12). But to know Christ is to be conveyed into a different mode of being in the world—a knowing other than the inherited form of knowledge that has its roots in the authorized version of right-mindedness. The philosopher of religion Rudolf Otto calls this "faith-knowledge," which enables the Christian knower to know things, see things, and understand things that supersede all other forms of knowledge.[13]

And finally, wisdom is not the stuff of secret or esoteric knowledge that is confined to the scholar's study or the philosopher's den but functions in the marketplace and at the city gate as a guide to action. As William McKane says: "Wisdom operates where the competition is fiercest, not so much the competition of other orators as men's preoccupations with those things which they take more seriously than listening to speeches, earning their living, making bargains, getting wealth, transacting local politics, settling disputes and other less gracious enjoyments. It is against all this that Wisdom has to compete."[14] Wisdom is a mode of confident action in the world that makes a difference to the way the world we live in works, and actively seeks to subvert the authorized version of right-mindedness which forms the default system that operates in the media and our educational institutions.

CONCLUSION

Such is the power and potency of Christ, and his appeal to the peoples of the world, that today there are people from all over the world in all sorts of corners in tribal Africa, industrializing China, the favelas of Latin America, and the jungles and teeming cities of Asia, who have passed up the wisdom of Confucius, the teachings of Lou Tzu, the pillars of Islam, the totems of tribal religion, and the sayings of the Buddha in order to

---

13. Otto, *Idea of the Holy*, 222.
14. McKane, *Proverbs*, 345.

drink deeply from the wells of Christian redemption which they believe has made them "wise unto salvation" (2 Tim 3:15 KJV).

In this chapter we have explored wisdom as a central pillar of the Christian faith. Sitting at Jesus' feet and learning of him is where this wisdom begins. Seeing from a Jesus'-eye point of view is how wisdom is practiced, and learning to live and love as Jesus commanded us is to become truly wise.

7

"I" for Imagination

"In the religious view of reality, all phenomena point toward that which transcends them" (Peter Berger).[1]

SEEING AND BELIEVING ARE dual aspects of the spiritual life. This connection makes imagination and faith intimate acquaintances. A believer's spiritual encounters with God, and the biblical stories that frame them, serve as a foundation for this arrangement. Let us now explore imagination's role in enabling spiritual believers to perceive the reality of God.

ENCHANTMENT

I am the eldest of six children. I am blessed to have five younger sisters. On the family farm where we grew up there were two houses: the larger, original weatherboard homestead with its tin roof and post-build verandas, and the smaller workman's cottage. My father's elder brother lived in the larger house with his wife and two children, while my father lived in the smaller house with my mother and their six children. A distance of about a hundred meters separated the two houses, broken by a number of large trees, a rough-hewn tennis court, and a children's sandpit. Halfway between the two houses was a smallish, gnarled, misshapen tree we called "jack frost." That small tree exerted a strange power over us as children. I don't remember when it first occurred to us that this tree was charmed. Perhaps it was on some foggy winter's morning when we looked across to the big house and saw jack frost hovering curiously

---

1. Berger, *A Rumour of Angels*, 94-95.

in the moving sheets of mist. I have a half-memory of playing outside with my two eldest sisters, at around age seven or eight, when we agreed that the strange misshapen tree with its missing limb and hollow section at its base was weird. On the one hand we chose it as our home base when we played tag, but on the other hand we were wary of it and approached it with caution. What was it about this tree that both attracted and repelled us? Was it inhabited by ancient nature spirits? To this day I still think about jack frost with a strange mixture of premonition and portent. Even as an adult I remain convinced that the tree was enchanted in some way.

Imagination (Greek *phantasia* or Latin *imaginatio*, both meaning "what is absent to the physical senses" and "to bring before the mind's eye something which belongs to past-time") is vital to human memory, reason, and creativity. As a primary generator of intuition, insight, and perception, imagination lies at the center of our human capacity to transcend the limits of our bodies. People whose imaginations function well seem to know where they are going in life, even when they launch into the unknown. Generally speaking, there are five kinds of imagination.

Imagination as *fantasy*. This form of imagination has a playful, unrestrained child-like quality to it. It escapes the limitations of human boundedness to inhabit the realm of fantasy. Some people may see fantasy as dangerous and mistaken, but artists and imaginaries understand it to be necessary for the development of a fully rounded self-awareness. True, fantasy can be egoistic (e.g., I want to fulfill *my* desires) or sinister (e.g., I make plans for revenge). But fantasy is a normal part of healthy childhood development, which continues into adulthood in the well-adjusted person. Playful imagination constructs castles in the air, but it also allows us to project forward into the unknown to create new possibilities for our lives out of, as yet, nonexistent materials. Fantasy is a strange but necessary admixture of playfulness and utopian longing. Unreal it may be, but it is a preparation for the coming of the real.

Imagination as *creativity*. This kind of imagination is the storehouse of images, expressions, and stories where human genius dwells. In order for humor, creativity, and artistry to break into full expression, we need a storehouse of generative energy. Without the capacity to generate new insights and capture fresh realizations, humankind languishes in a half-lit life. Our creative imagination is a critical aspect of self-awareness and self-expression that enables us as human persons—created in the image of God—to share as cocreators in God's ongoing creational and creative activity. People express themselves in myriad ways. Take music as an example. There are many forms and styles of music (e.g., classical, rock, folk, jazz, blues, country, folk, gospel, soul, fusion, metal, swing, and reggae). Clearly, creativity is important for our human lives.

Imagination as *intuition*. Intuition is a left-handed way of knowing. Call it perceptive, emotional, or innate, intuition enables us to engage with the mystery that accompanies our lives. We live in bodies we do not understand, we function in relationships that do not always make sense to us, and we use technologies that are not always self-evident. For the most part, our lives are not lived by cold reason but by warm intuition. We guess our way forward on the limited information we have available to us. Indeed, the role intuition plays in our imaginative lives is larger and more important than reasoned thought can know. This is also true of our spiritual lives, as we will discover.

Imagination as *reason thinking outside the square*. Believers in the rationalist era of modernity have sometimes accused imagination of being childish, irrational, and subjective. John McIntyre sums up this tendency in the statement, "intellect must rule over imagination."[2] But there are a lot of different ways of knowing. Many times our knowing is in the mind (factual), or in the heart (integrative), or through intuition (emotional). None of these are wrong, and all are right depending on the circumstances we find ourselves in. When we speak with our lover, feeling and emotion needs to be foremost. But when we sit at a university exam, factual knowledge comes first. Or when attending a family wedding, the bonds of relationship and connectedness come to the fore. There are many different kinds of knowing, and imagination has an important part to play in them all—depending on context.

Imagination as *enchantment*. Enchantment does not necessarily mean to "bewitch" (which is one possible meaning of the word). It can also mean to "impart a magical quality" (which is another, more friendly meaning). Enchantment—in the positive sense in which I am using it—is not so much to abandon one world for another as it is to superimpose the supernatural world over the natural world in order to supererogate (supercharge) them both. In today's world, many people have identified the "spiritual turn" made by our culture and recognize the reentry of spirit and the spiritual into human existence. For example, we are just

---

2. McIntyre, *Faith and Imagination*, 101.

as likely to find spirit-related "hooks" in advertising as we are to find sex, science, or success. But at the same time, few people have a clear understanding of what they mean by the spiritual dimension, and lack the language and concepts required to either take up residence in that enchanted domain or to communicate it to other people.

Earthly, physical people are more than the sum of their parts: we are made for heaven. But we must learn to activate the spiritual senses in order to navigate our way between the physical and spiritual worlds we know are there. This book offers a Christian understanding of life, the world and everything, to enable readers to either come to understand and inhabit the spiritual life for themselves; or to develop the reader's capacity to assist others in their spiritual journeys towards their highest potential.

The writer Ursula LeGuin has suggested that in the early part of the twentieth century "Americans were afraid of dragons."[3] By this she meant fantasy, science fiction, and epic stories were rejected in favor of reason and science, reflecting a deep mistrust of the imagination. Thankfully, the second half of the twentieth and the early twenty-first centuries have made up for the earlier loss of enchantment, by way of a virtual flood of creative works of music, art, science fiction, and Hollywood epics. In the current environment it is obvious that a re-enchantment of the Western spirit is taking place, so that once again fairies live at the bottom of the garden. The place of the imagination is now being reintegrated into the hearts, minds, and lives of twenty-first century citizens. The successes of J. K. Rowling's *Harry Potter* and J. R. R Tolkien's *Lord of the Rings* as stories which invoke the struggles of the human spirit, demonstrate the return of journey, mystery, and encounter with the supernatural in ways that the generations immediately preceding ours could hardly have imagined. As redemptive epics, these stories have become imprinted onto our psychological makeup. The realm of the magical and the spiritual are now firmly cemented in our cultural repertoire, even if there remains a good deal of ambivalence about the place and role of a specifically "Christian" spirituality, and how to negotiate one's way between the natural and the supernatural worlds. Yet the message could not be clearer—the Western world is no longer afraid of dragons!

---

3. LeGuin, in Fisher, *Inner Rainbow*, 6.

THE IMAGINATIVE EYE

There is a strong connection between the eye and the imagination. First, think of the arts. All great art forms—literature, theater, painting, dance, music, and cinema—engage the eye to one extent or another. Cinema, the digital Internet, and paint media (such as pastels, oils, and crayons) address the physical eye. Narrative-based literature addresses the inner eye of the imagination. Musical performance, while being in the first instance auditory, is also compellingly visual,—as is shown by the lavish costumes and sets used in opera productions. Anyone who reads Dostoevsky's *The Brothers Karamazov*, attends Shakespeare's *Macbeth* at the theater, hears Beethoven's Fifth Symphony, or sees a Cézanne masterpiece realizes that the arts are a powerful imaginative force. These works are the fruit of human imaginative ability, but they also provoke a powerful imaginative response in their audience. It is especially in the arts that we observe the connection between the eye and the imagination.

Second, think of poetry. Poetry belongs to the broader field of the arts, but for the purpose of exploration I have placed it in its own category. Poets and poetry have the power to name and evoke things through the power of language, things that are only half seen out of the corner of one's eye, but which are nevertheless real. William Dyrness has written a poetic theology that accounts for the entire Christian story from the first disciples to St. Augustine, to Dante, to Luther, to Evelyn Underhill, until now. Dyrness conceptualizes Christian faith in terms of it being a poetic reality.[4] The book rehearses the Christian story, understood as a kind of poetic development. Poetry (related to the Greek *poiesis*, meaning "to make") powerfully expresses themes related to the inner life, including the spiritual life. The poet Samuel Taylor Coleridge differentiated between the "primary" and the "secondary" imaginations.[5] The primary imagination as conceived by Coleridge is the basic "human capacity to see and organize stimuli from the world around us." It is the power to recognize "providence" and to exercise grateful thanks and appreciation for the beauty and power of the natural world. By contrast, the secondary imagination engages with God's grace and recognizes itself as standing in the presence of God—*coram Deo* ("before the face of God"). Poetry is uniquely able to imaginatively translate the written verse to the percep-

---

4. Dyrness, *Poetic Theology*, 38.
5. Discussed by Levy, *Imagination and the Journey of Faith*, 9–10.

tive eye, because both are directly related to human life and meaning. It is through poetry that we discover the point of contact between the imagination and the eye.

Third, think of science. Science also has the potential to be a work of the imagination. Researchers dream and imagine into the future in order to create cures for diseases such as smallpox, polio, and hepatitis that ravage their fellow humans. Through concerted inquiry researchers are able to overcome obstacles to locate those all-important cures. Presently, medical scientists are imagining cures for HIV, cancer, and diabetes, and are pouring hundreds of thousands of research hours and hundreds of millions of dollars into discovering such cures—none of which yet exist or can be seen by the naked eye. Yet they can be perceived by the imaginative eye through a process of anticipation, intuition, felt need, and shared humanity.

Fourth, think of society itself. In *A Secular Age*, Charles Taylor sets out to investigate what happened to the secularization hypothesis prominent in the intellectual discourse of the Western world over the past fifty years and to identify the causes of the spiritual revolution currently unfolding in our society.[6] One of the concepts Taylor has contributed to the public discourse is the notion of the "social imaginary." The idea of a social imaginary relates to the kinds of ideas that operate in the background of a society's consciousness. Taylor identifies three kinds of social imaginary: First, what is taken to be normal, taken-for-granted knowledge in the minds of everyday people. In other words, potatoes to the Irish and apple pie to Americans. These are the unexamined ideas that form the repertoire of conventional knowledge, beliefs, and actions. Second, the ideas that operate in the public square, and how these ideas are held and promoted in the media, education, and politics. This is where public opinion is formed and expressed in the public space. And third, how opinion changes in the public mind, and the kinds of mechanisms that allow ideas to transition from "what is" to "what might be." No culture and no set of ideas, however well entrenched, are ever sheltered from change because cultures and ideas are always in dialogue with other sometimes competing and sometimes complementary visions of what is real. Society itself is constructed from the gossamer threads of its imagination. It is the end product of the constant making and remaking of webs of meaning. When a society's imaginative life is

---

6. Taylor, *Secular Age*, 2007.

strong, the society itself is healthy. When its imaginative life is weak, it suffers from a failure of the imagination and gives way to mediocrity and banality. The poet Paul Claudel described the nineteenth century as an era of a "starved imagination," and the same can be said of the mid- to-late twentieth century.[7] Failures of the imagination are observable in periods of political confusion, during economic disarray, and where injustice reigns.

MacNeile Dixon said this most clearly when he placed imagination at the center of human life in general and spirituality in particular: "If I were asked what has been the most powerful force in the making of history, you would probably judge me of unbalanced mind were I to answer, as I should have to answer, metaphor, figurative expression. It is by imagination that men have lived; imagination rules all our lives. The human mind is not, as philosophers would have you think, a debating hall but a picture gallery."[8]

Imagination is a powerful force in the human spirit. By projecting our inward hopes, dreams, and desires outwards onto the canvas of life, we are able to anticipate, create, and work toward a quality of life that supersedes and replaces the quality of our present existence. The eye of the imagination, or *the imaginative eye*, has a central place in the way we live our lives and the stance we take towards our very existence.

THE SPIRITUAL IMAGINATION

Faith is a kind of imagination. Faith locates resources necessary for its own inner life in those Spirit-given sources of knowledge available to it (e.g., Jesus'-eye point of view perspective, the visionary text of the Bible, the translucent quality of the kingdom of light, and the covenantal form of knowing that is uniquely its own.) Faith endeavors to constitute a better world than the one bequeathed by the flat, one-dimensional natural world. As a form of imagination, faith dares to question the status quo offered by the authorized version of right-mindedness through the media and culture of consumerism. Before faith can leap to the new realities it discerns in the other dimension, it asks the question: "Is the world *really* as the spin doctors say it is?" It also asks: "Is there anything better

---

7. Claudel, in Schindler, "Truth and the Imagination," 521.
8. Dixon, *Human Situation*, 65–66.

on offer than the acquire-consume-satiate ideology blaring out of every TV set and championed in every shopping mall?" Whenever one form of faith is operative, its default set of values and assertions call into question (even doubts) the truthfulness of other visions of the real. Indeed, Christian believers find themselves watching and listening to a different story and looking through a different vision that offers a supernatural-redemption-transformation hermeneutic. Let's explore each of these in turn.

First, the *supernatural*. The reality our bodily senses report to us is one-dimensional. Individuals, through our physical senses of touch, sight, smell, taste, and hearing, engage with the surrounding world. There is no doubt that the things with which we engage in the physical world, are real—but that is not to say there is not something more. Spiritual vision looks through the appearances of the everyday world with the imaginative eye to see the more substantial world of the kingdom of God. The believing soul reaches to grasp and touch the realities it sees there. Having claimed the resources of heaven for their own, saints learn to apply the resources of grace, goodness, blessing, and restoration to their embodied, earthly lives. Spiritual vision allows us to grasp eternity and bring it to bear on the ordinary, everyday world such that the normal state of affairs is overturned. Here, ordinary people become immortal, and ordinary time is superseded by sacred time. The spiritual imagination recreates the world so that all ground is holy, every bush burns, grace tinges the brown world green, and God's fingerprints are seen everywhere.

Often our problem is the inner voice of doubt that accuses us of making unsubstantiated, unnecessary, and imaginative leaps of faith into the unknown. We are tempted to ask ourselves the question, "Why bother?" And we are tempted to believe the lying voice within us; that is, until we remember that every position people take and every confession they make (whether spiritual, religious, scientific, economic, or political) proceeds by faith. How is this? None of the presuppositions people use to justify the claims they make about what is real in the world can ultimately be proven. Everyone lives by faith! Christians, Buddhists, atheists, freethinkers, hippies, and hobos. *Everyone!* Even people who subscribe to the authorized version of right-mindedness live by faith. As Christians we are willing to acknowledge this reality and to affirm that the foundations of our identities as followers of Christ are supernaturally informed but naturally activated. It is supernatural faith that elevates and authenticates our natural existence—in the name of Christ. The life of heaven is recreated on earth through an imaginative new society that looks like, sounds like, tastes like, and acts like the kingdom of God on earth. But it is still faith (or imagination grounded in reality) that informs our perception.

Next, the *redemptive*. Some unbelievers get all knotted about the idea of sacrifice and divine violence that belong to the Christian redemptive story. But what they fail to realize is that it is God directing violence toward himself, not humanity. This needs to be placed in perspective. As I have written elsewhere, Christianity is a *healing tradition*.[9] We are very aware of the three healing traditions that currently function in the Western world: (a) traditional Western medicine's naturalistic-biological-curative approach; (b) complementary medicine's holistic-systemic-harmonizing approach; and (c) the psycho-therapeutic tradition's developmental-psycho-somatic-integrative approach. People often understand Christianity to be a religious tradition, but it can just as easily be understood as a healing tradition, using a fourth approach to healing; namely (d) a remedial cosmic-restorative-redemptive approach. It doesn't take much of an imagination to see this.

Jesus came healing. "The blind receive their sight, the lame walk, those who have leprosy are cured, the deaf hear, [and] the dead are raised" (Matt 11:4–5). The book of Revelation depicts the end of history as a time when "He [God] will wipe away every tear from their eyes. There will be no more death or mourning or crying or pain, for the old order of things has passed away" (Rev 21:4). According to the Christian account of history, Jesus' crucifixion, resurrection, and ascension put into action the necessary reconciliation between God and his broken creation, restoring it to its original creative design. On these terms then, Christianity is as much a healing tradition as it is a religious tradition. As a healing tradition, redemption does not simply atone for personal sin and resolve internal problems; redemption brings about the restoration of the whole order of creation. Christian theology claims that creation provides a harmonious existence for humans, comprised of physical well-being, social well-being, and spiritual well-being. Redemption brings about a *re*-creation in order to correct the fall, linking physical and existential wholeness with spiritual, ethical, and relational holiness.

9. Devenish, "Contribution of Spirituality," 2012.

The Christian understanding of history is that God's engagement with human suffering does not produce more human suffering. Rather, it produces voluntary divine suffering which is intended to heal and restore a broken humanity to its creational originality.

And third, the *transformative*. Transformation is about positive and upward change. The most basic transformation of the Christian spiritual life is conversion. Jesus taught about the "new birth" in John 3, identifying it as the entry point into the spiritual life. Conversion brings with it a divinely informed vantage point from which the new convert is able to see higher, further, and clearer than ever before. A friend of mine reported that "As Christians we see with different eyes; we hear with different ears; we feel with different hearts; and we think with different minds."[10] The reality is that every adult, youth, or child who has ever undergone a dramatic spiritual experience knows at some deep place in their existence that their lives have been changed in a fundamental way. From that moment on their old way of thinking and knowing ceased to provide a satisfactory explanation for the way things are in the world. Having stood on holy ground, it is not possible for converts to go back to their earlier life. Everything has changed, nothing remains the same. They find themselves in a new place. And this new place brings with it a new world, with a new perspective, and a new form of Spirit-guided logic.

Such is the transforming power at work in the believer's life. While new disciples retain their customary name, personal history, and appearance, nevertheless they are transformed into new people whose vision is transposed to such an extent that they know differently, understand differently, and perceive differently. And this "knowing otherwise" radically alters their capacity to imagine the world in new ways because the palate of idea materials available to them is greatly enlarged.

SOME FAMOUS IMAGINARIES

I want to conclude this chapter by exploring the lives and imaginations of three Englishmen who lived between the late nineteenth and the mid-twentieth centuries: George MacDonald, J. R. R. Tolkien, and C. S. Lewis. George MacDonald (1824–1905) was a Congregational

---

10. Tony van Keule, private conversation in Bunbury, Western Australia, November 2000, with permission.

minister who trained at the Highbury Theological College (London) between 1848 and 1851. Being a sensitive soul more given to romantic wanderings than to tightly constructed Calvinist theology, MacDonald always remained somewhat aloof from the institutional church, but he took seriously the care of the souls around him. Today, MacDonald is remembered chiefly as a writer of fiction and fantasy, and is particularly well-known for his imaginative works such as *Phantastes*, *The Curate's Awakening*, *The Princess and the Goblin*, and *Lilith*. He became mentor to some of the most significant writers to influence the twentieth century, such as G. K. Chesterton, J. R. R. Tolkien, C. S. Lewis, W. H. Auden, Mark Twain, Madeline L'Engle, John Ruskin, and Lewis Carroll. To give the reader just a taste of MacDonald's acumen as a writer, consider the following on the topic of imagination:

> When therefore, refusing to employ the word *creation* of the work of man, we yet use the word *imagination* of the work of God, we cannot be said to dare at all. It is only to give the name of man's faculty to that power after which and by which it was fashioned. The imagination of man is made in the image of the imagination of God. Everything of man must have been of God first; and it will help much towards our understanding of the imagination and its functions in man if we first succeed in regarding aright the imagination of God, in which the imagination of man lives and moves and has its being.[11]

Although he was not much recognized during his lifetime by his contemporaries for either his ministry or his writing, MacDonald became increasingly recognized after his death as something of a literary celebrity.

MacDonald influenced J. R. R. Tolkien, who became professor of Anglo-Saxon language at Oxford. Tolkien was keen on studying ancient languages and mythologies, as well as writing poetry and fiction. He found inspiration and encouragement in MacDonald's fictional fantasy writings. Tolkien wrote in the *Lord of the Rings*: "It reminds me very much of Bilbo . . . 'It's a dangerous business, Frodo, going out your door,' he used to say. 'You step into the road, and if you don't keep your feet, there is no knowing where you might be swept off to.'"[12] Tolkien has become a major contributor to the reintroduction of the imagination of

---

11. MacDonald, *Dish of Orts*, n.d. Author italics.
12. Tolkien. *Lord of the Rings*, 87.

the Western psyche through story, narrative, and epic tales. One begins to imagine that we have not yet heard the last of Tolkien.

C. S. Lewis was also significantly influenced by McDonald. Lewis was professor of English literature, also at Oxford, and was a member of the Inklings group along with Tolkien, Charles Williams, and others. Lewis is best known for his *Narnia Chronicles*, but also has wider appeal through his contributions to medieval literature, ancient mythology (as a literary critic), and Christian apologetics. Lewis was said to have picked up a copy of MacDonald's *Phantastes* to read while on a train trip and soon became convinced of the value of MacDonald as a writer. He reported that a "bright shadow" had leapt off the page as he read, which he later described as a new quality of "holiness."[13] He also described that moment as the time when his imagination was "baptized," coming to believe that imagination was not simply another human faculty amongst many. Rather, he preferred to describe imagination as "the organ of meaning."[14] Lewis's exposure to the Christian imaginative literature, along with the encouragement of Tolkien, led him to acknowledge that imagination was in fact the birthplace of his faith in Christ.

> All the books were beginning to turn against me. Indeed, I must have been as blind as a bat not to have seen, long before, the ludicrous contradiction between my theory of life and my actual experiences as a reader. George MacDonald had done more to me than any other writer; of course it was a pity he had that bee in his bonnet about Christianity. He was good *in spite of it*. Chesterton had more sense than all the other moderns put together; bating of course, his Christianity. Johnson was one of the few authors whom I felt I could trust utterly; curiously enough he had the same kink. Spenser and Milton by strange coincidence had it too. Even among ancient authors the same paradox was to be found. The most religious (Plato, Aeschylus, Virgil) were clearly those on whom I could really feed. On the other hand, those writers who did not suffer from religion and with whom my sympathy ought to have been complete—Shaw and Wells and Mill and Gibbon and Voltaire—all seemed a little thin; what as boys we called "tinny." It wasn't that I didn't like them. They were all (especially Gibbon) entertaining; but hardly more. There seemed to be no depth in them. They were too simple. The roughness and density of life did not appear in their books . . . The upshot of it

13. Lindsley, "Importance of Imagination," 1.
14. Ibid.

all could nearly be expressed in a perversion of Rowland's great line in the *Chanson*—"Christians are wrong, but all the rest are bores."[15]

Lewis could never hide the fact that he regarded MacDonald as his master teacher, admitting that he had never written a book in which he did not quote him in some way. Lewis's commitment to the importance of imagination in human knowing and identity was only surpassed by his belief in the primacy of imagination for the spiritual life. It was, after all, in the place of the imagination, not in the place of dogmatic preaching or theology, that Lewis himself was able to meet God. This provides us with an important clue that imagination acts as the place where spiritual seekers encounter God on their journey of discovery we call spiritual pilgrimage.

In summary of this section, we have discovered that some of the greatest thinkers of the late nineteenth and early twentieth centuries drew a strong link between the imagination and the spiritual life. Their literary contributions were significantly strengthened by this discovery in their own lives, as was the quality of the contributions they made to civic thought and spiritual practice. They were, in their own ways, spiritual imaginaries whose use of the eye of faith has left a legacy of perceptive and imaginative faith that continues to exert a discernible influence on Western Christians even today. Although they are dead (so far as this life is concerned), "yet they speak" (Heb 11:4).

CONCLUSION

This chapter has explored the themes of enchantment, the imaginative eye at the center of spiritual imagination, and several notable imaginaries. We explore these themes to discover one key truth—that faith is a kind of imagination, and the kinds of things we discover there do not always fit easily with the authorized version of right-mindedness promoted by our culture. If we draw from a well somewhere within ourselves to find positive resources for our lives (e.g., memory, beauty, love, hope, and anticipation), it requires no great leap of faith for us to draw imaginatively from the treasure trove of Christianity's invisible assets. Those invisible assets are the love of God, the human and divine life of

---

15. Lewis, *Surprised by Joy*, 202–23.

Christ, the hope of salvation, and the presence of the kingdom that surrounds us. Even if we cannot see these things with the physical eye, the eye of faith imaginatively apprehends those realities and enables us to become residents of that magical kingdom that is the kingdom of God.

The Australian poet Andrew Lansdown wrote of creativity and the imagination:

> Surely it is true that God intends human beings to be creative. How could it be otherwise, since we are made in his own likeness? We are his image-bearers. This means that because he is rational, we are rational; because he is moral, we are moral; because he is creative, we are creative. God's image in us explains why human beings and humans alone among all earth's creatures compose music, paint paintings, sculpt sculptures, direct plays, choreograph dances, write stories, and so on. We see clay and imagine a vase; we see stone and imagine a human body; we see color and imagine a painting; we see movement and imagine dance; we hear sound and imagine a symphony; we think words and imagine a story. And our creativity is not limited to arts and crafts but applies equally to science and technology—in fact the whole of human life is a life of imagination and creativity. This is inevitable because the great Creator made us in his own likeness.[16]

I imagine Lansdown has it right.

---

16. Lansdown, "Fantasy and its Place," 2006.

8

Toward an Understanding of Christian Spiritual Vision

> *"Before your very eyes Jesus Christ was clearly portrayed as crucified"* (Gal 3:1b).

IN THIS CHAPTER I want to draw some of the most important ideas explored in this book together to provide a spiritual theology of the eye of faith. As we proceed, we need to be aware that we are touching mystery here. Because the spiritual realm is never fully disclosed to us, and because only those whose eyes have been awakened can see, there is always more to see, know, and understand than what we presently imagine. But that is precisely the point here: it is not possible to completely grasp the invisible, nonphysical realities on which our faith rests. But it is possible to learn how the eye of faith functions and how to look in such a way that the spiritual realities that are seen by the eye of faith are brought to the foreground of our awareness as observable phenomena. The spiritual theology of the eye of faith explored in this chapter pays more attention to the believing soul's mode of seeing, rather than to what is seen in the beatific vision. Those with eyes to see, let them see.

CONTEMPLATIVE VISION

In 1983 the Roman Catholic priest and writer Henri Nouwen visited L'Arche in Trosly, France. Founded in 1964 by Jean Vanier, L'Arche is a community for people with mental disabilities. In successive years Nouwen made several return visits and on each successive visit some thoughtful housekeeper placed a different icon on the table in the room where he stayed. During each visit Nouwen spent long periods of time looking at those icons, praying and developing his contemplative vision. He described those visits as the times when he learned to see spiritually. One of the icons he spent time with was painted in the fifteenth century by Andrei Rublev for a church in the Russian city of Zvenigorod. This icon has come to be known as the *Savior of Zvenigorod*. The icon depicts the face of the risen Christ in a dramatic azure blue set against a wheaten parchment background. The icon had once been lost and was only rediscovered in 1918 under some steps in a rural barn. It had languished there for several decades. Because of its antiquity, the image had become worn and weather beaten. Yet Nouwen discovered that out of the icon there shone the most dazzling eyes. Despite its history of loss and rediscovery (which paralleled Jesus' own pain and suffering), Jesus' weathered face conveys a remarkable identification with the suffering of the Russian people. Nouwen began by looking intently at the icon, but as he looked he discovered something. He discovered that even as he was "seeing Christ," he felt he himself was being "looked at."[1] He discovered that "Jesus is all eyes."[2] Nouwen wrote:

> Seeing the Christ of Rublev is a profound event. Through the ruins of our world, we see the luminous face of Jesus, a face that no violence, destruction or war can finally destroy. We see his tender humanity asking us to lay aside our fears and to approach him with confidence and love. We see his eyes, eyes that penetrate not only God's own interiority but also the vastness of human suffering throughout all history. Thus, seeing Christ leads us to the heart of God as well as to the heart of all that is human. It is a sacred event in which contemplation and compassion are one, and in which we are prepared for an eternal life of seeing.[3]

Some Protestant readers may not feel comfortable using icons as a part of their worship, but Nouwen's encounter with the Savior of Zvenigorod icon is an instructive case study in contemplative vision. Icons are bridges that invite us to cross over from this world to the other dimension. Through a series of unexpected encounters with these icons, Nouwen learned to exercise his spiritual eye through a process of intentional looking. He was deeply moved by what he saw in the face of Jesus.

---

1. Nouwen, *Behold the Beauty of the Lord*, 45.
2. Ibid., 53.
3. Ibid., 56.

And he learned that intentionally looking at Jesus often makes us acutely aware that Jesus is looking back at us. "To be is to gaze and be gazed at."[4]

When the Apostle Paul addressed the Galatian Christians using the words, "Before your very eyes Jesus Christ was clearly portrayed as crucified" (Gal 3:1b), he did so in the full knowledge that neither he nor any of the Galatian Christians had ever seen Jesus in the flesh. Yet he adopted the language of the optics of faith, drawing his readers' attention to how they had come to visualize Jesus in their minds'-eye as the Son of God, and the one who had justified them. Their coming to see Jesus as Lord and savior, and to place their faith in him, came as a result of Paul's preaching and teaching. While Jesus was not physically present, he had nevertheless become the center of the Galatian church's worship and contemplation. His real presence deeply affected the inner lives of his worshippers. But through neglect and counter teaching, the Galatian believers had suffered a loss of focus, which invited Paul's pastoral rebuke for their lack of faith and their spiritual blindness. Although they began their Christian lives with faith and trust, through neglect and fear they were tempted to return to the Jewish law and the works of the flesh. The trophy of obedience is clarity of spiritual vision; but the result of neglect is spiritual blindness.

These two case studies—one from the first century and one from the twentieth century—both highlight the importance of spiritual vision. In particular, they demonstrate how effectively the act of spiritual contemplation makes Jesus present to the believing community, but also how susceptible that vision is to neglect and a loss of focus. We learn that vision and the spiritual life work hand in hand with each other. The spiritual life is a visual life, and faith-filled believers are constantly engaged in the act of seeing. As the philosopher A. N. Whitehead defined it:

> Spirituality is forming a vision of that which stands beyond, behind, and within the past influx of immediate things; something which is real, to be explored by a close attention to our immediate world, and yet waiting to be realized; something which is a remote possibility, and yet the greatest of present realities of our life; something which gives meaning to all that passes and yet for ever invites our apprehension; something whose possession is the ultimate good, and yet as that beyond our life demands an ongoing quest; something which embeds us in relationships with

---

4. Camilleri, "To Be is to Gaze and Be Gazed At," 2009.

others, and yet at times will require a journey in solitude; a vision that makes us participants in the unfolding of the universe, yet ever mindful of and haunted by the horizons beyond that unfolding, provision requiring the exercise of the mind, heart and body, and a vision replete with consequences for action.[5]

Historically, when Christians have spoken about spiritual vision, they have used words like *contemplation* and *discernment*. Contemplation is a central feature of Christian prayer in which the worshipper intently calls to mind the presence and gifts of Jesus through a process of meditation, contemplation, and immersion in the depth reality that these things represent. Contemplation in its older sense is often understood as something mystical, where the pray-*er* actively seeks a form of divine union with God through beatific vision. Contemplative prayer has often been practiced by monastic individuals and communities. In its more recent usage, contemplation has broadened to become part of centering prayer or as a part of spiritual retreat. Similarly, discernment was once referred to as the "discernment of spirits" which sought to discern good from evil and to identify God's fingerprints in the life circumstances of spiritual seekers and retreatants. Spiritual directors often use discernment to distinguish between "consolation" and "desolation"[6] experiences in order to assist directees to find the places where God is active in their lives and to adjust their attitudes and responses appropriately. More recently, the concept of discernment has broadened to include moral and vocational choices that face people in their increasingly complex lives.

Generally speaking, *vision* can be defined in different ways. First, vision is the capacity to see things through the physical eyes. In this sense vision or sight is one of the foremost physical senses. Second, vision is what is observed—or the thing itself. It is the object that catches our eye. Third, vision is something seen not with the physical eyes but reconstituted in the memory of the human observer. This might be of a beautiful place you once visited, or the face of a deceased parent, or a long-lost friend. Fourth, vision can be an aesthetic vision of beauty, such as Monet's famous painted garden at Giverny in France. Fifth is strategic vision, a term that is sometimes used by institutions and organizations. This kind of vision refers to a corporately owned, idealized future state and is generally accompanied by a series of steps to facilitate a business

---

5. Whitehead, *Science in the Modern World*, 275.
6. Larkin, "Discernment of Spirits," 115–16.

or congregation's forward movement toward achieving the wished-for future outcomes. Sixth is the gift of foresight, which is a vision often bestowed on particular individuals who are described as visionaries. Seventh, a vision can be something shown to us from outside ourselves, such as destiny or a dream of a future event. Eighth is a beatific vision, a term that is known spiritually and is in the literatures of Christian theology. Beatific vision generally refers to a believer's imaginative vision of Christ, either in this life or in death following his or her entry into heaven.

But there is a further category of vision that we can identify. In this category, vision is a regenerated and elevated knowledge of God that is seen and known by the believing soul as a result of his or her life-transforming encounter with Christ. Here, the believer possesses a spiritually derived knowing faculty that looks for all the world like a set of spiritual eyes. It has been our goal in this book to develop this category of vision, taken to its ultimate end point. At the heart of Christian discipleship is an activated form of vision, given to the believing soul as a form of standard issue at their conversion, which enables him or her to see into the mysteries of the spiritual life. This vision is an important faculty of faith that is observable in the lives of Christians in every place and time.

FACULTIES OF FAITH

When Henry Nouwen visited L'Arche, he learned to see spiritually by looking intently at the *Savior of Zvenigorod* icon. Nouwen's disclosure of how he came to see spiritually represents a single instance of when an individual learned to exercise spiritual vision. So there are questions that need to be asked about Nouwen's experience: How exactly did he do that? How can I do that in my life? How does this apply to an entire congregation? And what are the implications for a whole life of spiritual seeing, rather than one or two brief instances?

There is a single answer to these many questions. Learning to use the faculties of faith, which are given to us by the Spirit of God, ensures that an individual Christian (in a particular instance or over the course of a lifetime of faith) and an entire congregation of believers (wherever and whoever they might be) can learn to exercise the form of spiritual vision that operates through the eye of faith that has been the focal point for our study. The following section will explore the faculty of faith that operates through the eye of faith.

But first we have to address a potential blind alley when it comes to the eye of faith. One of the most common events people report about their eyes are floating spots. So-called floaters are small particles of blood, tissue, or debris floating around in the eye fluid that cast shadows across the retina. These become visible to us only when they cross our line of vision. When we move our eyes or refocus on a new object or optical field, they seem to follow our line of sight. Spiritually speaking, it is possible to become distracted by spiritual "floaters" that cross our spiritual line of sight. Spiritual floaters might be such things as psychological flotsam and jetsam, unresolved sin, a willful eye practiced in wanderlust, or a particular pattern of belief or doctrine that invades our awareness and blinds us from seeing anything else. Being distracted by spiritual floaters would be like focusing on the bug on the windscreen rather than the oncoming traffic or, a tourist looking only at the bus on which they are riding rather than looking at the beautiful scenery all around them. In order to overcome these momentary distractions and to learn to see spiritually, we need to pay attention to the spiritual eye as our primary mode of seeing. When we learn to exercise a sustained spiritual gaze and to maintain proper spiritual perspective and focus, we are then able to look on the face of Christ, which is the foremost characteristic of the inner life of the believing soul.

At the crisis known as the new birth or conversion, the Christian believing soul receives the faculty of spiritual sight. This is a gift given by the Spirit of God to new believers to equip them with the capacity for spiritual vision. Using this faith faculty the new believers are able to navigate their way between and through the double realms of the physical and spiritual worlds. It is by means of this spiritual faculty that believers become seers of the supernatural, hearers of mysteries, tasters of divinity, and touchers of heaven. At conversion the newly arrived believer has their common, everyday, garden-variety understandings of the world radically changed. These understandings of the world have been variously described by scholars as a "universe of meaning," "plausibility structure," "master narrative," or an "inward working model." It is these life visions that drive and inform peoples' thoughts, beliefs, actions, and intentions.

Conversion and insight are intrinsically linked. Richard Peace has suggested that conversion itself is prepared for by a new form of insight: "Insight drives conversion. Without insight there literally cannot be conversion. It does not matter if that insight is slow or sudden, or if the insight comes by means of careful sifting of the facts so as to reveal truth or by means of a flash of creative intuition. It does not matter if the precipitating cause is internal or external . . . But there must be some trigger, otherwise the turning point cannot even begin. Conversion begins with insight into one's own condition as it concerns God."[7]

But Dallas Willard brings us to the point of what conversion actually produces in us. He says:

> Genuine conversion is a wrenching experience. It involves the breaking down of a worldview and the acceptance of a different set of ideas. It can cause deep damage to the most intimate of relationships, as Jesus warned (Luke 12:51–53). It can seem like madness or wickedness, precisely because it goes against what everybody takes for granted. And in many parts of the world Christians are persecuted today because they threaten the dominant idea-system of their culture. Jesus himself confronted and undermined an idea-system and was killed for it. But he proved himself greater than any local idea-system. Indeed, his ideas transcend specific cultures because they constitute a complete and consistent worldview. The idea system of Jesus works anywhere, any time. But it involves radical change.[8]

At the moment of spiritual transformation, the new believer receives a faith faculty that can be likened to a map, a lantern, a sextant, or a compass. The spiritual eye of such an individual is not only awakened so that it can see into the unexplored lands of the spiritual realm, but it begins to make out shapes and to see things previously unknown and unseeable. This faith faculty enables believing souls to navigate their way between the two worlds they live in. The images of map, lantern, sextant, and compass are imaginative capacities that enable believing souls to go outside themselves in order to enter into the Jesus-centered, biblically shaped, redemptive universe that is carried by the Christian salvation story. This enables them to navigate their passage forward within the larger spiritual universe on the basis of their ability to maintain their

---

7. Peace, *Conversion in the New Testament*, 54.
8. Willard, *Renovation of the Heart*, 70.

location as measured against the horizon of Christ who is their spiritual north. In dangerous times and unmarked territory, having an on-board spiritual GPS ("global positioning system") is of utmost importance.

In the history of Egyptology, archaeologists have uncovered vast quantities of cuneiform script, but there was a time when they were unable to read it because they lacked any interpretive key to understand the script. Frustratingly, they found themselves unable to interpret the mysterious cuneiform writing of the ancient Egyptians. The way forward was blocked. Fortuitously, they discovered a small molded clay tablet with a sequence of interpretive keys that unlocked the meaning of the images and sarcophagi inscriptions found among the ruins of the Egyptian pyramids. Today we know this little stone as the Rosetta stone. On the basis of one small stone, an entire universe of meaning was unlocked.

In the same way, Christian believers who have at their fingertips the imaginative perceptual capacities we have identified as a map, a lantern, a sextant, or a compass can navigate their way in their spiritual realm using the eye of faith. Many Christian disciples experience themselves having received a ready-made, fully operational awareness of the spiritual realm. They do not know how it got there; they just know it has an important part to play in their spiritual lives. On the basis of their encounter with Christ, the work of the Spirit within them, their reading of the Scriptures, and the teaching contained in their faith tradition, believers are able to interpret the spiritual realities before them.

But this faculty of faith is not indestructible or inviolable. Like a candle in the wind it is extremely vulnerable. If left unattended it dies down to a sputtering flicker. But if carefully tended, it flares up like an intense flame. This is where spiritual formation is crucial. Left to their own devices and without careful teaching and communal support, believing souls flounder and become lost in the confusing spiritual matrix. But believing souls who are appropriately nurtured and properly supported tend to grow towards Christlikeness and maturity. Churches that provide high levels of spiritual nurture to their adherents through intentional teaching, based on careful biblical exegesis and positive reinforcement through role modelling, tend to be good at producing disciples who have a positive spiritual polarity. Ministry leaders who know how to feed their congregations and to keep them on the growing edge tend to enjoy high levels of community integration and a shared sense of purpose. Churches of well-taught, well-fed, and well-focused saints do not find it difficult to identify people who want to be positively engaged in worship, prayer, mission, and social justice ministries expressed through acts of compassion. And as a consequence, those churches experience less turmoil and conflict in their faith community than is otherwise the case.

New converts are a blessing to any church. Look carefully and you will see that their conversion to Christ has produced in them a measurable change in life direction, in how they think, and what they "see." Conversion "reconfigures the coordinates by which all of life is interpreted."[9] As they develop the practices of routine Bible reading, attending Christian worship, and participating in activities such as prayer and witness—all of which enable them to experience a closer sense of the presence of God—their capacity to see spiritually increases. Believers who associate with other believers and who receive positive teaching and faith reinforcement, tend to grow rapidly in their knowledge of what God requires of them, how to please God, and have a growing confidence about what constitutes right living as citizens of the kingdom of God.

AN EIGHTH-DAY SPIRITUAL THEOLOGY

People suffer from four great delusions regarding the spiritual life. The first is self-reliance (e.g., that it is somehow possible to live without God, and to solve the great psychological and spiritual problems of life from our own human resources without reference to God). The second is religiosity (e.g., that religious observance—rituals, practices, and performances—actually impress God, as if God could be tricked into thinking that our actions are true reflections of what is in our hearts). The third is universality (e.g., that all spiritual teaching, regardless of its origins, allows humans to progress up the mountain towards God). All roads, so this line of argument goes, lead to God. And the fourth is Gnosticism, or spiritual elitism and special knowledge. I want to pay a little further attention to this latter delusion.

The gnostic heresy has played a large part in the life of the Christian church from the second century onwards. Gnosticism recognized the problem of human fallenness and separation from God but tried to find

---

9. Hall, "Choosing Life or Second Life?" 19.

a way to deal with it and to "get out of jail" by manipulating the natural order via hermetic formulas, esoteric knowledge, and abstruse incantations. Gnosticism refused to submit to the Christian gospel (what C. S. Lewis might call God's magic), which appealed to the work of Christ on the cross on the behalf of a fallen humanity, and instead tried their own self-help remedy. Similar to alchemy—where ordinary elements such as rock and stone were (supposedly) turned into extraordinary elements such as gold, silver, and jewels—Gnosticism is a self-directed, do-it-yourself way of salvation that bypasses the teachings of Jesus and depends on other, lesser ways for deliverance.

Readers familiar with this territory may have suspected that, at times, this book has verged on the precipice of Gnosticism. But I wish to argue that a healthy, biblically derived Christian spirituality contains a certain amount of enlightened spiritual knowledge, vision, or insight at its heart, and that this is in fact by God's design. Believers know things unbelievers don't know. Faith gives them eyes and insight to see it. Being a disciple of Christ means to sit at his feet and to learn of him. But discipleship is not Gnosticism, because it is Christ-dependent and not self-dependent; therefore, it cannot be said to be gnostic. It can, however, be said to be mystical in the sense that its central insights are not available to everyone, only to those who have had their spiritual eyes enlivened and awakened to the "mystery of the gospel" (Eph 6:19), under the guidance of the Holy Spirit. True Christianity is not gnostic, but it does contain special knowledge that is available to all those who are spiritual and who, through faith in Christ and through baptism, have been initiated in the mysteries of the Way of Jesus.

At the center of the Christian confession is what can be called the language of an eighth-day theology. The concept of the eighth day brings together the two most important concepts in Christian spirituality: creation and redemption. At the close of this chapter, I want to draw these two primary elements together in a significant way. We understand creation to refer to God's calling of the natural order into being through divine fiat (or "command"). In the first six days, God creatively imagined the universe, called it into being, He saw it, and called it good. And on the seventh day he rested.

Many Christians ignore creation, preferring instead to spend all their waking moments thinking about redemption, as if creation and redemption were two distinct processes in the mind of God. But salvation is nothing more than a *re*-creation; a restoration of the created order that has been ruptured. The fall is creation disrupted: Adam and Eve were put out of God's garden and God's presence. Redemption fixes that disruption by restoring the relationship, reinstating and returning the godlike human creatures back to their original creational place in the garden and into the bosom of God. Redemption is creation righted.

Redemption is a sequence of events that moves from Adam and Eve in the garden; to their exclusion by God's command because of their disobedience; to mankind's attempts at self-elevation through their own strength as exemplified at the Tower of Babel; to God's election of the nation of Israel as a working model of redemption (the shop window of what a restored, reconciled, and redeemed people looked like); to Israel's ignoring of their elect status before God; to the arrival of the prophets whose task it was to deliver the word of the Lord; to the arrival of the person of Jesus who preached the kingdom of God and whose voluntary surrender to crucifixion for political sedition and religious blasphemy provided the atoning sacrifice that turned away the wrath of God and reconciled mankind back to himself.

But to this point redemption had only been announced. Its arrival is partial, patchy, and incomplete. But there is a day coming when it will arrive. The Christian gospel—however poorly and incompletely it is preached, disseminated, and acted out—actually points to this fulfillment. It is a point in history where all the revolutions of change, struggle, pain, and waiting find their fulfillment. This is the point of arrival and accomplishment. While it is true now that "the end of all things is at hand" (1 Pet 4:7), when the eighth day comes these things will find their fulfillment. The idea of realized eschatology points toward this now-but-not-yet tension in which Christians find themselves waiting now in anticipation of the joyous fulfillment of the Christian hope then, which will be "Christ among you, the hope of glory" (Col 1:27).

The eighth day theology we are discussing here calls the church to live *now* in the same manner it will live *then* in the presence of God, in the truth of Christ, in the power of the Spirit. It calls us to bring the two worlds of the present and the future, our broken humanity and our redeemed humanity, together to overlap each other in order to be totally and utterly renewed. This is the goal of an eighth day theology. An eighth day theology requires us to enlarge our exilic consciousness to the point where we can see clearly through the eye of faith the coming day of

Christ, and to commit to living now in the light of the coming reality of the Day of the Lord. This is the ideal of the saintly life. It is a life in which believing souls find a way to integrate their physical, enworlded bodies and their spiritual, supernatural beings into a single, Christ-filled person that all at once appears to be knocking on death's door (in our physical bodies) and knocking on heaven's door (in our spirits). Neither world is rejected as being evil or unnecessary; both worlds are embraced with equal passion and conviction. *"Therefore we do not lose heart. Though outwardly we are wasting away, yet inwardly we are being renewed day by day . . . So we fix our eyes not on what is seen, but on what is unseen. For what is seen is temporary, and what is unseen is eternal"* (2 Cor 4:16–18). *Maranatha*: come Lord Jesus!

CONCLUSION

There is so much more to say about the spiritual life, in general, and the eye of faith in particular. But every good thing must come to an end. Let me conclude with three thoughts. First, the writer James Loder has offered a far-reaching statement about vision: "A vision of the Holy is a vision of reality so magnificent that the human self longs for the Holy to be all in all, totally transforming existence in the fullness of its light and being."[10] A spiritual theology of the eye of faith calls us to reflect deeply on *who* sees, *how* they see, and *what it is* they see. Second, the act of spiritual seeing is intended to help us overcome the blight of "spiritual floaties" and "double vision." It does so by teaching us how to use our capacity for second sight. And third, the spiritual faculty given to us at our new birth is not to remain undeveloped. As J. B. Phillips once wrote, "It would appear that one of the great reasons for us living on this planet at all is that we may learn to use and develop this [spiritual] faculty."[11] After all, we are destined to spend eternity looking into the face of God in an unclouded vision of his splendor and glory.

---

10. Loder, *Transforming Moment*, 90.
11. Phillips, New Testament Christianity, 38.

9

Discipling the Eyes

"I ask . . . the God of glory to make you intelligent and discerning in knowing him personally, your eyes focused and clear, so that you can see exactly what it is he is calling you to do" (Eph 1:18, *The Message*).

LET US REVIEW SOME of the key points made in this book in order to highlight some implications for congregational servants and local churches in their ministry priorities and activities. I have argued that the eye of faith is of critical importance to the Christian spiritual life at the present moment in history for five basic reasons: (1) the age of the eye presents Christian disciples with multiple distractions; (2) the soul is a seeing prism predisposed to both soul sleep and acute sight; (3) the essence of faith is seeing from a Jesus'-eye point of view; (4) a primary task of the church is to train the eye to see Christianly; and (5) the process of optical therapy forms an essential part of spiritual formation. Let us begin the review.

THE AGE OF THE EYE PRESENTS CHRISTIAN DISCIPLES WITH MULTIPLE DISTRACTIONS

A metaphor here can help guide our thinking. A group of friends arranges to meet at a local cinema on a Saturday afternoon for some relaxation and entertainment. It's been a long year and summer vacation is around the corner. The mood is relaxed and playful. After haggling over what movie to watch, they agree on their preferred choice. They visit the snack bar and purchase enough popcorn and fizz to keep them happy for the afternoon. They settle in their favorite seats, not too close to the front and away from the noisy back rows, to await the start of the movie. They make it through the ads okay. But as the lights dim and the first flickers of the movie begin, something very odd happens: multiple movies begin showing at the same time. Suddenly, flashing before their eyes are all the movies listed to show on that day; but even more strangely, there are scenes from every movie they had ever seen, all playing at the same time! The scenes flashing before their eyes become surreal. The scenes swirl and images blur. The boundary between storylines and lifelines converge. Instead of engaging in the serious business of chilling out on a Saturday afternoon, the group of friends are confronted with Hannibal Lector, Lara Croft, the Three Stooges, the Joker, Neo, and Scarlet O'Hara, and more! At first, the cut and paste nature of the scenes is intriguing, even intoxicating; but as the scenes speed up, wonder and adventure give way to fear and terror. The list of storylines goes on and on. They hear the sound of reality cracking. The lines between art and insanity distort. Faces contort. Reason aborts.

This Saturday afternoon activity was not what these friends had intended to experience. The reeling and wheeling effect of the "society of spectacle" left some in the group feeling elated and hyperstimulated. But it had demanded that they abandon themselves into multiple alternate realities where there was no solid place to stand. Their momentary exhilaration had come at a cost, the loss of their true selves. They had lost their personal freedom by allowing themselves to become imprisoned in the stories that now carried them to unknown and unwelcome places. Others in the group were left in a state of toxic shock. The murder and the blood, the lust and the violence, and the disconnection and dissociation had left them feeling nauseous. The bliss of a relaxing Saturday afternoon had become their worst nightmare.

The age of the eye in which we live is a cinematic age where multiple competing visions of reality play simultaneously. The task of Christian disciples is to separate out the biblically defined and divinely sanctioned vision from among other competing visions and to maintain it as their primary point of reference. Holding that vision as their internal working model and conforming their lives to it, even as other competing visions of reality surround them, is their primary calling. Their task is to maintain a single eye, a single vision, and a single commitment to Christ in a world where plural options exist. Christians are people who have always chosen to follow Christ over all other available options. They are people of a singular eye.

THE SOUL IS A SEEING PRISM PREDISPOSED VARIOUSLY TO SOUL SLEEP AND ACUTE SIGHT

In one church where I pastored, I got to know a couple who owned an impressive home cinema. The husband had worked for years in the audiovisual industry and had developed a notable specialization in the field. So he did what one might expect him to do: he built a hi-spec professional cinema in his home, complete with a giant widescreen TV, the highest quality professional sound system he could find, and thirty plus speakers including bass speakers positioned under the chairs where the audience sat.

I make mention of this impressive home theater for one important reason. From a spiritual perspective, every Christian believer has a home cinema showing within them. No matter where they are, who they are, or what they are (in society, in their denomination, or in their church), the soul within each believer functions as an inbuilt personalized movie theater. Playing within each individual is the supernatural, redemptive, and transformative narrative of the Christian story. It is set to play on permanent loop—the same storyline played over and over again. The spiritual life is primarily a visual life, and the soul is a remarkably responsive seeing, knowing, and perceptive prism. The goal of the spiritual life is to embrace Christ who beckons us. Christ cannot be seen with our physical eyes, but he can be readily seen by the imaginative eye of faith. The soul's deepest longing is not only to know him and embrace him but to be known and embraced by him. Previously we have said that the soul is "all eye." And right there, in hundreds of millions of lives, the Jesus story "plays" out as the guiding story that defines the way the world is supposed to be.

Mary Oliver has observed, "This is the first, wildest, and wisest thing I know . . . that the soul exists, and that it is built entirely out of attentiveness."[1] The soul is a wild thing in that it is free to make its own choices. Because God assigns freedom and authority to it, not even he can make the soul choose for him. The soul must itself desire to make that choice, and then build that relationship out of its own freedom. On the one hand the soul is capable of the most acute spiritual insight. It has the divine spark folded into its fabric at creation, and is awakened at redemption through the work of the Spirit. It is incredibly adept (when

---

1. Oliver, "Low Tide," 34.

it is awake) at reading the cosmic drama in which it is engaged. It is attentive to the spiritual realm, even if it must peer through the gloom as through a mirror darkly (I Cor 13:12, KJV). Even new Christians, who have had little teaching, have a partly formed, ready-made understanding of what Jesus asks of them when he says, "Come, follow me." More mature Christians are able to see heaven opened," and to discover the mind of Christ. But the soul, as Mary Oliver observed, is a wild and willful thing that finds it easy to rebel and assert its own counter freedom. Indeed, the soul suffers from a form of spiritual attention deficit syndrome, and struggles to hold its gaze in the midst of the tournament of competing visions. The soul is often unwilling to take every thought captive to Christ (2 Cor 10:5). The human heart also suffers from a sleeping sickness from which it needs to be awakened. The normal state of the human heart is dull; it too needs to be awakened and aroused.

THE ESSENCE OF FAITH IS SEEING FROM A JESUS'-EYE POINT OF VIEW

As I write this, my wife and I have just celebrated our thirty-fifth wedding anniversary. All those years of working, serving, living, loving, studying, and raising children seem to have gone by very quickly. But at present we are going through a new season in our lives. For reasons of work and family, we are temporarily living in different cities. But thirty-five years of love and mutual commitment is a long time. I know her better than anyone else on earth, and I can call her face to mind any time I want to. And when I do, I remember how much I love her and how happy she makes me feel. The distance that temporarily separates us does not mean that our relationship has ended or that our marriage is in trouble. It is simply what it is—a temporary interruption to what has been and will continue to be an amazing marriage to a wonderful person.

Faith is like that. It can produce in the Christian "seer" images and representations—usually constructed from scriptural material, memory, the meaning of spiritual experience, and personal encounter—that shape and define his or her life. With just the smallest exertion of spiritual energy, such a believer can bring into the mind's eye the call of Jesus through the single, focused, undimmed eye of faith. Seeing the invisible and responding to what they find there is what spiritual people do best. And they do it because they have been given access to a new dimension of reality that has inducted them into new vistas of knowing, being, and *seeing*. They have been made privy to a special kind of knowledge that does not originate with themselves but out of the mind of God. In order to sustain this transformative vision, this luminescent wisdom in the midst of the multiplicity of visions and distracting images, they must hold their gaze. Anyone who has ever played the "stare game" will know how difficult it is to do this. The aim of the game is to outstare one's opponent. The first person to blink or look elsewhere loses. Maintaining our spiritual vision in one long, sustained look is at once tiring and exhausting; but it is also energizing and exhilarating. On those occasions when we do turn our eyes away to look at other things, we are prompted to remember our calling and to return our gaze once again to the face of Christ. To look inwardly is to see the face of Christ; to look outwardly is to see from a Jesus'-eye point of view.

THE CHURCH'S PRIMARY TASK IS TO TRAIN THE EYE TO SEE CHRISTIANLY

People must be taught how to see. If the eye (that which sees), sight (our mode of seeing), and vision (what is seen) are central (but often neglected) elements of the Christian spiritual life and practice, it is a wonder we have ignored them for so long. If, as the writer to the Hebrews teaches, "faith is being sure of what we hope for and certain of what we do not see" (Heb 11:1), then the eye of faith is a central feature and foundational element of the contemporary saint's moment-by-moment walk through this world which is overshadowed and underwritten by a reality greater than what the saint sees with his or her physical eyes.

Because of the prominence of the invisible, nonmaterial world for the spiritual life, and the difficulty of accessing that non-material reality, the eye must be trained to see. The task of training the eye of faith is one of the most important tasks for the local church. Training the eye of faith occurs in the midst of the faith community's worship life, through teaching, through spiritual direction, through appropriate and wise pastoral guidance, and through the modeling of faith by congregation leaders.

Training the spiritual eyes of faith seekers, and of those who already have faith, is a first-order task of the Christian church. It is the primary responsibility of its priests and ministers, elders, and teachers, worship leaders and youth leaders. In particular it is the responsibility of parents to guide their children toward an understanding of the faith they profess as a family. Parents need to be both encouraged and resourced in their role as educators of their children toward the knowledge of salvation. That is to say, anything the church does is in addition to the foundational work of what parents say and do in the home.

One of the most important but neglected ministries of the church is teaching people how to see spiritually. Spiritual seeing is central to discipleship; and teaching people to see spiritually can only be done properly in the context of the Christian faith community, including families.

OPTICAL THERAPY FORMS AN ESSENTIAL PART OF SPIRITUAL FORMATION

Spiritual formation seeks to grow people into the image and likeness of Christ. It is a progressive process of guided instruction that intentionally seeks to fashion the lives and characters of disciples into the image of Jesus Christ. It applies to both leaders and followers, as well as to individual believers and the corporate body of the church. Spiritual formation is an important contributor to spiritual growth. It takes place through a process that normally involves the three activities of information, formation, and transformation. In order for the believing soul to embrace Christ and to know themselves as being loved by God, a fundamental *re*-cognition must first take place in their inner person. *Change in the outward life always arises and originates from change in the inward life.* What constitutes transformation in the context of the Christian spiritual life is a determined, sustained, Christward change that begins in the heart, that affects the eye, and which proceeds outward into every part of the life.

In our visual age, optical therapy forms an essential part of spiritual formation. The writer Esther Meek wrote of the need for a kind of optical therapy that offers to "correct" and revise the kinds of authorized versions of right-mindedness that people bring into their faith lives from their backgrounds.[2] In place of the multiple versions of reality that swirl around us, the church needs to offer a curriculum for the soul that provides and teaches an alternate vision of reality from the Christian point of view. This point of view consciously begins and ends with the Jesus'-

---

2. Meek, *Loving to Know*, 3–30.

eye point of view perspective that identifies him as creator, sustainer, redeemer, and Lord. All other visions of the real are to be submitted to his sovereignty and Lordship. Jesus is the bringer of light, the centerpiece of God's wisdom, and the primary agent of God's redemptive drama. As C. S. Lewis once said, *"I believe in Christianity as I believe that the sun has risen. Not only because I see it, but because by it I see everything else."*[3]

If Christian ministry is to be renewed, if Christian discipleship is to be reprised, if Christian spirituality is to be recovered, and if Christian identity is to be reframed, the eyes of the faithful must be refocused. I am suggesting here that Western churches develop a workable curriculum for the soul. It must be well resourced, intentionally prepared, cooperatively shared, and properly implemented in every local congregation through a process of disciplined and sustained spiritual formation. This process needs to teach believers, old and new, how to see Christianly, how to understand the dimensions of the Christian world in which they reside. They must learn how to make use of their faith faculty of spiritual sight. Anything less will be less than Christian.

Christians need to "learn how to love the right things," and so spiritual teaching and mentoring are a first-order priority in the church.[4] The same applies when it comes to seeing the right things. Discipling the eyes is the task of every ministry leader, and leaders must invite their congregations to become followers of Jesus through biblical preaching, imaginative teaching, and life-giving mentoring. Their lives must willingly mirror his life and reflect the qualities and values of the kingdom of God. The end result will be to subvert the ingrained values of this world. If Christianity is to be effective in our visual culture, a catechism of the eye needs to be put in place. Believers will need to be systematically trained in the use of the eye of faith. Only when they see heaven can they move into it as their new personal address and perceptual residence. All forms of Christian education have as their central impulse the desire to deepen disciples' commitment to, understanding of, and participation in the Christian redemptive narrative.

And so the end has come. What have we said? That in a society of spectacle, Christians are to remember that we are a society who wear Jesus spectacles, and that learning to believe rightly in a culture of unbelief, or many beliefs, necessitates our learning to employ the eye of faith

3. Lewis. *They Asked for a Paper*, 165.
4. Leonard, *Becoming Christian*, 25.

rightly. "Jesus set forth the vision of the kingdom of God as the apocalyptic vision of a coming world that calls us to see beyond the present."[5]

> Earth is crammed with heaven,
> and every common bush is on fire with God;
> but only he who sees takes off his shoes;
> the rest sit around it and pluck blackberries.[6]

---

5. Ibid., 67.
6. Browning, "From Aurora Leigh," 152.

10

Focusing Your Spiritual Eye

Mind your inner eye.

THE "POTENTIALS" OF THE EYE OF FAITH

ATTENTIVE READERS WILL HAVE noted that this book has been written from a somewhat idealized point of view. It may give the impression that Christians are picture-perfect saints who have a direct line of sight to God. It may also give the impression that there is no winter in the church and that all darkness, sin, and obfuscation have been removed. Let's be honest and just admit that, if anything, this book is overly Pollyanna-ish. I still haven't decided whether that is a good thing or a bad thing. If it were a good thing, it would enable us to discover the "potentials" of the Christian spiritual life found in the promises of Christ, as many of the saints before us discovered for themselves. If it were a bad thing, I admit that overstating the potentials without acknowledging the credibility gap between Christ's high calling and the church's meager performance is incredulous, naive and self-deceptive.

But because we live in an undisciplined and undisciped age, shaped by the values of the consumer society and the amoral culture around us, we need to be reminded of the high-water mark of Christ's calling on our lives. Setting the benchmark of what is actually possible to achieve—God being our helper—is important. We need to remind ourselves that we have not yet arrived at perfection. Being invited to either discover (for the first time) or remember (if we have been this way before) that we are called to live a life that is in Christ is a good thing. We have been invited "with unveiled faces [to] contemplate the Lord's glory, [having been] transformed into his image with ever-increasing glory, which comes from the Lord, who is the Spirit" (2 Cor 3:18). It seems best to take this invitation seriously. God seems to mean it. If the truth claims made by Christians are anywhere near true (and I believe they are), then turning God down doesn't seem like a very good idea.

If I have painted the sea blue, it is with the intention of reminding us that while Christ calls us to a higher life he also provides the resources to allow us to get there. We cannot do it all ourselves—that is not possible. And we should not ask God to do it all for us—that is presumptuous. No, the spiritual life is a partnership. We are God's fellow workers, both in the spiritual life and in ministry. There is God's part and there is our part. I do not want to overinflate the Calvinist-Arminian distinction, but when it comes to salvation I am a Calvinist, relying on Christ to elect me and place my name in the Lamb's Book of Life. And when it comes to living the spiritual life I am a Wesleyan Arminian, recognizing that I have a part to play in staying saved, remaining sanctified, and keeping my eyes on Christ.

We have to acknowledge to ourselves that not everyone who confesses Christian faith lives consistently with the teachings of Christ, or honors God in their daily living. Somehow this shadow side of Christianity must be acknowledged. There are some "ugly Christians" amongst us; and if we are honest with ourselves, there may even be an ugly Christian living in each of us. For those of us who profess faith in Christ, there are corners of our faith lives that remain uninformed, unformed, and unfinished. The Apostle Paul used the metaphors of a garden plot and a building site (1 Cor 3:9) to describe disciples in formation. What characterizes both is that they are often messy and are frequently works in progress.

So with regard to the potentials of the eye of faith and all that it can behold, we are often inattentive to our spiritual lives; we often suffer from *acedia* (or lack of spiritual desire), and we are frequently blinded by sin. Perhaps it is time to recover our "first love" for Christ and renew our commitment to follow him. There will be a cost to discipleship we may yet have to pay. The work of committing or recommitting comes with a price tag attached. Heart work—I have found—is always hard work. But that cost ends up being a bargain when compared with the cost of turning away from Christ, or remaining a lukewarm Christian. Taking steps toward renewing our followership after Christ requires that we renew our vision of Christ by opening up the eye of faith within us. We cannot love Christ if we do not know him or are not able to discern him at work in our interior lives or in the world at large. Renewing our commitment to follow Christ means we will have to be attentive to our inner eye—that part of our spiritual lives which enables us to discern good from evil, right from wrong—in order to discern the presence of Christ and our own simple desires. Learning to see again, spiritually speaking, is the first step to renewing our faith. Ours is an era when there are many visions in the world, and we must learn to discern where Christ is at work.

A POSTMODERN CONFESSION

Bruce Haddon has written a post-enlightenment, postmodern confession that captures the substance of historic Christian teaching. But at the same time, it also reflects the experience of Christian believers whose lives have been impacted by their secular-humanist education and by the authorized version of right-mindedness that surrounds them in their everyday life worlds. I think his confession wonderfully captures the tensions—and offers the possibilities—that comes from living as a Christian by the values of an unchanging gospel in a changing and conflicted world.

The View beyond the Window[1]

I *know* the universe could not come from nothing. Even if it started with a bang, something created that, or created the rules that did. That ultimate creator could not have come from nothing either, so has always existed. I call him God and "he" not because he needs a name or is male but because that's how my language works. I know this ultimate creator is personal because I am personal and God could not have created personality if it were beyond him. Therefore I *know* the universe has an ultimate creator who has always existed and that he is powerful and personal.

I *believe* a personal God might want to exercise his personality with other personal creations in the universe, of which I am one. Believing

---

1. Bruce Haddon, "A Postmodern Confession," Sydney, July 2007 (personal correspondence, used with permission).

that doesn't make it true. But the mental step of believing changes me and sensitizes me to new possibilities outside tangible realities. No other truth I have found so far has rendered unbelievable the idea that a personal creator may wish to relate to me in terms I can understand, therefore I *believe* he relates to me.

I *experience* a relationship with God even though we exist on vastly different planes. Pets relate to me in ways more animal than human. Little children relate to me in ways more childlike than adult. But I can understand how they are thinking and know and enjoy them on a level similar to the way they know and enjoy me. I retain my superior knowledge when I do this, but I curtail it to relate to a simpler being. This corresponds to how I believe God relates to me and how I know I relate to God.

I *express* my relationship with God in the English language and in Western concepts and ideas. I could use others if they were in my head but these are the ones I have. It doesn't mean God speaks English or thinks in Western concepts, it means I do. I also know my language and concepts are not ultimate truth and are a narrow bandwidth in the context of human history and human understanding. Therefore I *express* a relationship with the small part of God I can access on my limited human understanding. My expression of that relationship is shaped by what I am and who I believe God is. While I am human, it's the best I can do.

I *imagine* a picture of God via human images and metaphors. They give God a form I can understand. I believe mankind is unique among living things because of this capacity. Some mental images of God are my own, others are borrowed from believers old and new who willingly offered them because they shared their experience of God and had enough imagination to give it form. At times in human history believers thought their imagined picture of God was the total picture. At times in my childhood I thought the same. Post-enlightenment and post-childhood I now understand this mental form of God is a window into the truth. I *imagine* the view beyond the window but I cannot see it fully. And I do not fall in love with the window.

I *choose* to commit to the mental model of God I have created from my available knowledge and the limits of my present thinking. That doesn't mean I created God. It means he created me with a capacity to know him via a mental model of him that changes in line with evolving human knowledge and my Christian journey. Ancient believers considered God created the firmament, the domelike structure that contained the sky. Today we can fly there and confirm their knowledge of the universe was inadequate. But they were not wrong to believe God created it. God is not bound by the mental models or figures of speech we create to understand him in our time in history or stage of life, but we necessarily are. No believer's simplification is the whole truth and neither is an unbeliever's dismissal of our simplifications. Unbelievers question the shortcomings of human reductions of God. They are welcome to question them but wrong to think that if they have dismissed someone's concept of God they have also dismissed God. If they chose to seek God they could develop a concept that reveals God to them. I *choose* an over-simplification of God rather than the over-simplification that says there is no God. My reduction of God connects me to a wider reality too vast for me to otherwise understand.

I *am inspired* by a Bible that tells me something of how God related to people before Christ and after. Since I belong to the second half, the New Testament has far more to teach me. The New Testament informs my relationship with God and equips me to do for my time what New Testament believers did in theirs. I cannot adopt their pre-scientific knowledge and they cannot access my post enlightenment concepts. But neither of us needs to, since we have the direct experience of God in common. That experience, inspired and informed by the Bible, is more than just the words in the Bible since the power of the words comes from the relationship not the other way around. I could be inspired by God without the Bible and some Christians have no other choice. But since I have the Bible, a relationship with God inspired and informed by it is my only choice. This experience drives me to a deeper study of the Bible which better informs my experience, but the reality of the experience creates the power of the Bible. Therefore I *am inspired* by the Bible because it is a window to God. But it's the view through the window I seek. I *love* the historical character of Jesus I find in the Bible. He is the best human expression of God I know and I form an extraordinary bond with others who feel the same way. God as I understand him would not withhold knowledge of himself from those who lived before Jesus or are separated from him today by culture or context. So Jesus' role as a window to God would be available to them even if they sought it but were never told his name. Jesus is called Prince, King and God's Son as a tribute by the people who know him. I recognize in the language of those who lived in Jesus' time the same timeless wonder I experience in Jesus today. Jesus is not all of God because all of God can't fit into any human body or mind. He is a working model of as much of God as can be compressed into human form. I can imitate that, but could never imitate God. Therefore I *love* Jesus for who he is and the way God is uniquely reflected to me through him. He is a window to God and closer to the view beyond the window than anyone or anything else I can know.

I *share* the story of Jesus and the church and this story creates a common bond with others today who are part of the same unfolding story. This story is also sometimes strangely attractive to people who, prior to my sharing it with them, considered themselves non-believers. I have been there, alas too rarely, when in others the human side of reality extends miraculously to accommodate the super-normal reality of God. I imitate in my lifetime the choices Jesus made in his to the degree they can be applied to such a different place and time. I model myself on my understanding of his insights and encourage others to do the same. I try to please God by being more like Jesus and I experience remorse when I fall short of my understanding of his expectations. I want to know Jesus better, follow him more closely and grow to be more like his example. I become a better person and achieve more for others and society when I do. Because I *share* Jesus' life and the story of the gospel inwardly and outwardly people call me a Christian. The experience would not change if it were called something else. There is nothing supernatural about the word, or any word. There is everything supernatural about Jesus and the way he invites me to share his life.

I *connect* with God in a range of conscious and semi-conscious mental processes, the most obvious of which is prayer. My prayers are usually in English because that makes the most sense to me, but God would hear me in any language or no language. I can pray in thoughts not words and it still feels the same. Prayer does not bring me good luck, but I feel more equipped for life's randomness and vagaries and more joy at its wonders and a deeper attachment to the universe and my fellow humans because I pray. Since I cannot go back and re-live my life without prayer, I can't measure the difference it makes. But I want to connect with God this way and don't intend to stop. So even though I can't hear his voice through my ears I never stop listening for it in my mind. Therefore I *connect* with God through prayer. I know prayer changes things because I'm something and it definitely changes me.

I *glimpse the sacred* via experiences that are not clear enough to replace the other ways I seek God but too clear to be explained as ordinary events. A change of attitude for the better that occurs without conscious effort, so that I do not remember changing my mind until after I have. Coincidences of such utter improbability that even a skeptic would be tempted to think someone had ordered their occurrence. A sudden rush of relevance for a Bible verse I stumble upon apparently at random. An impulse to make a small change that ends up fundamentally altering significant events. A feeling I am loved that I cannot attribute just to the people who love me. Homesickness for a life beyond death even when I have never seen the other side and cannot know for certain there is one. An insight that comes into my head with such speed that it seems to be there all at once and I then I think it out at the pace of normal thought. A compassion for the unlovely and a desire to forgive people I would normally find unforgivable. These glimpses are given the description of the Spirit of God living in me. That expression is just words but the reality is more than words. I cannot glimpse the sacred through someone else's eyes or glimpse it for someone else. Thus this uniquely personal experience cannot prove that I *glimpse the sacred* but it is confirmed at a deep level to me that I do.

Therefore I *am a Christian* because I know the universe has a creator who is powerful and personal. I experience a *personal relationship with God* via human images although the truth is more than I can imagine. I am inspired and informed by *the Bible* in which I also encounter *Jesus* whom I love for the way he reflects God back to me. I share *the Jesus story* which bonds me to other Christians and liberates others to see beyond their previous limitations. I connect with God through prayer and *prayer changes things*. I *glimpse the sacred* via experiences that cannot be explained as ordinary events and I attribute these experiences to the *Spirit of God* in me.

For these and other reasons I *am a Christian*. It is a living reality in my direct experience. Whatever the reality is outside my direct experience I cannot know. But I hope to know it in full once I no longer need this frail body with its human limitations. What else I will see I await with hope and joy. But this is true: while I lived I saw the view through the window and called him my creator and my friend.

THREE PRAYERS

In closing I want to invite you identify which of the three categories of *saint*, *servant*, or *seeker* you belong to (perhaps you belong to more than one, or none?), and to pray the prayer that belongs to each below. These prayers are designed to enable you to make a new beginning in your spiritual journey. If these do not suit—pray your own prayer.

A Saint's Prayer

Lord, I pray for your
Spirit's *illumination* in my life.
Help me not to be so spiritually blind
so self-dependent, so inconsistent
so prayerless.
Teach me to pray once again
to feel your presence
to desire you deeply
and not fall victim to the authorized versions
of right-mindedness all around me.
Help me to re-engage
with my spiritual life
to start again.
Give me a hunger for you
let me see you face-to-face;
enlarge my soul
teach me to take responsibility for my spiritual life
how to feed myself from your Word
through prayer, in commitment and sustained godfaring.
And help me to learn how to nurture the spiritual lives of others
beginners, fellow travellers, those ahead of me
as we together make our journey home to you
our life source, our redeemer,
our friend.
Amen.

A Servant's Prayer

Master,
I began so eager, so earnest, so vibrant
now sometimes I feel so tired, so weary
I feel like I have spent and spent
but have forgotten how to replenish, renew
the well of spirit within me.
Take the scales from my eyes Lord
give me your set of glasses
so I can see
as you see.
Help me to grow beyond the place
of irresponsible parenthood
bringing spiritual children into the world
then leaving them to starve
their souls wasting away.
I have
engaged in the thrill of winning people to faith
but have been careless
prayerless
in feeding and nurturing
their souls
to grow from
shrivelled up, to up-sized, to giant-sized
I confess, I recommit
I renew.
Give me a vision of your mountain
so I can the climb it—right to the top.
So I can see you
face to face
eye-to-eye.
My Lord
my friend.
Amen.

A Seeker's Prayer

Jesus
are you there?
I'm so new at this
I feel awkward
tripping over my own two feet.
But I feel like I've been looking for you my whole life
I want to come closer
I want to connect
I want to see your face
I want to see through your eyes so I can understand
your "take" on the world.
If there is a way
I'd like to take it
If there is a life
I'd like to live it.
There's a living room
somewhere here inside
do you want to move in?
I need to start again
I need some help
to run my life, to make some decisions
to find a place I can call home.
My eyes, Lord;
open my eyes
I want to see
you.
Amen.

Appendix

ON METHOD

FOR THE REGULAR READER, method can feel obstructive; it gets in the way of understanding. But for the scholar, method underwrites what we can know. I have included this brief appendix on method to indulge the scholars among us, and to reassure the nonacademic reader that a trustworthy schema underlies and underwrites the contents of the book.

Method has two primary tasks: first it verifies and validates any claims made in any argument; and second it provides a language and a means of expressing the topic under discussion. Method makes meaning accessible. It provides the framework for meaning that helps us interpret the information in front of us. In this instance, the phenomena we have explored is the *eye of faith*: what it sees and how it sees. Method adds clarity and depth to our field of vision.

The spiritual life has three central moments to it. Each of these moments forms the substance or building blocks of spiritual experience. The first moment is encounter. Encounter is the astonishing and unexpected meeting with God. It is unpredictable in nature, and has a raw, unprocessed edge to it. Because of the radical and transformative nature of our encounter with God, it is often difficult to describe and to understand. Method draws from other peoples' encounters with God (scriptural and historical) to provide a logic and order to spiritual encounter that, in turn, helps us understand the hidden impulses and life forces at work deep in the soul. The second moment is response. Most often, our response to the God encounter is expressed through worship, prayer, service, and consecration. Something this big demands all of me; my whole life! Understanding and describing such a totalizing, whole-of-life response demands that we apply something more to it than everyday language and thought forms. Nothing else could possibly be adequate to the task. Method provides tried and tested signposts and measures, so that we know when we are on safe ground and when we are in dangerous territory. And the third moment is the struggle to understand our encounter with God and the response that follows. We ask ourselves what just happened, and what does this mean for my life? Method replies: here are the pathways other people have travelled before you, here are some ways of understanding the transforming experience which has just shaken your life, and here are your options. Trustworthy spirituality does not look for new innovations or create untried and untested avenues. Instead, it looks for the old paths, well-signposted by previous travelers who have found the way to the city of God. Those paths always lead new travelers higher and deeper at the same time.

It is for these reasons that method is of such great importance to the spiritual life. It ensures that, instead of offering random descriptions and reactionary diagnoses, we are able to place spiritual experience in its proper context thus allowing us to accurately observe, describe, and analyze the core elements of the spiritual life on its own terms. Spiritual experience requires a proper method to ground it in a reasoned and reasonable environment; but it must be a method that respects and nurtures the spiritual life as a valuable component of human life, and as a proper response to the Divine call.

So, with those things in mind, I have chosen to apply four different kinds of method in this book. The first kind of method is spiritual theology. Spiritual theology is the branch of Christian theology that attempts to understand and interpret the religious experiences of individual persons and entire faith communities. Instead of discounting it as lunacy (as the secular mind is tempted to do), or imposing established orthodox doctrines on it (as the dogmatic religious mind is tempted to do), spiritual theology holds that the encounter with God and our response to it are of first-order importance. The impulses that most define a religious tradition are not the settled and static state it defaults to (e.g., Israel at rest in the promised land, or the settled parish churches of Christian Europe). What exerts the greatest defining influence on a religious tradition, and those people who make their journeys of faith inside it, are the tumultuous moments of encounter with God that live on in the memory of the people as their sacred touchstone, constantly to be retouched and reexperienced (e.g., Israel's deliverance from Egypt; and for Christians the coming of the Spirit at Pentecost and the dynamic Spirit-filled communal life of obedience that followed). Spiritual theology provides an approach to spiritual experience that values it and seeks to understand it on its own terms, without casting the jaundiced eye of sceptical disbelief towards it, or imposing overly ordered tradition-based understandings upon it. Spiritual theology makes sure we focus on the right thing.

The second kind of method I have chosen is a psychospiritual perspective. My long-term interest in the human person standing in the Divine presence has meant I have needed to find a mechanism to help me unearth the inner drives and motivations at work in the control center of consciousness. The psychospiritual method enables us to look inside the thought processes and interior consciousness of the believing soul. If anything, spiritual experience amplifies and enlarges everyday personal experience. I have focused on the eye of faith as my preferred observation point. This approach enables us to look inside the self-understandings and ecstatic moments that characterise spiritual experience. At its inception, psychology (derived from two Greek words: *psyche*, meaning "the soul," and *logos*, meaning "words about") was initially concerned with the functioning of the inner life; but subsequently, psychology has come to refer to the pathologies of the mind. Now, once again, psychology is being used for its original purpose to pay attention to the life of the soul. I am indebted to my colleagues in the Australasian Centre for Studies in Spirituality (who specialize in psychological, clinical, and therapeutic approaches to spirituality) for their guidance and assistance in managing the psychological apparatus. I have gained insights into a variety of psychospiritual resources, such as John Bowlby's attachment theory and the operation of internal working models in the inner life, both of which offer valuable tools for understanding the believer's attachment to God. A psychospiritual approach enables us to bring the inside outside—meaning we can get to look at the origins of the inner drives and motivations of believing souls, and to compare them with their outworking through behavior and actions.

The third kind of method I have selected is phenomenology. My doctoral work was in the phenomenology of new religious knowing in the context of Christian conversion. In its simplest form, phenomenology can function as a stethoscope to the soul which enables outside observers to look into the inner consciousness of the believing soul and to come to an understanding of what it sees at work there. Although I have not used the technical language of phenomenology in this book, the method and concepts of phenomenology soundly underwrite everything expressed in this work. Phenomenology ensures that we have a way of "observing" the soul and its operations.

The fourth kind of method I have selected is an aspect of theology known as reception. Many Christians understand the idea of God's self-communication through revelation. God's habit of showing himself to his creation, culminating in his most powerful revelation of himself through his Son Jesus Christ, is universally known and widely accepted. What is not so well-known is the other side of the coin: reception. Reception refers to the human being's act of receiving God's revelation of himself into his or her life personally, and the kinds of changes and alterations of belief, practice, and significance this provokes in the individual's inner consciousness. At a time when the "turn to the subject" has taken hold of our culture, reception has taken on a greater significance. It allows us to locate ways in which believers receive the gift of eternal life into their own lives. The Roman Catholic Church understands reception in terms of the *magisterium* of the Church and the *sensus fidelium* (the sense of the faithful) that generate the teachings of the Church and define its mission in the world as God's divine agent in human dress. My approach in this book is less concerned with the ecclesial center of the church and more concerned with the conscious center of the human person. To that end my concern is for the *sensus fidei* (the faith sense) at work in the life of the Christian believer.[1] Reception is the important place where the heart of God and the heart of the human respondent meet.

These then are the four kinds of method I have chosen as the interpretive keys for this book. Because this work is intended for a more general audience, I have tried to ensure that these methods are present throughout the work but do not impose themselves unnecessarily on the text. In their own ways, each of these methods have steered us safely through the mysteries of the spiritual life to reveal the realities that lie within.

---

1. Rush, *Eyes of Faith*, 2009.

Bibliography

Barclay, William. *Turning to God: A Study of Conversion in the Book of Acts and Today.* London: The Epworth Press, 1963.
Barnhart, Bruno. "One Spirit, One Body." In *The Participatory Turn: Spirituality, Mysticism, Religious Studies.* Edited by Jorge N. Ferrer and Jacob H. Sherman, 265–92. New York: State University of New York Press, 2008.
Berger, Peter. *A Rumour of Angels.* Garden City, NY: Doubleday/Anchor Books, 1969.
Biderman, Shlomo. *Scripture & Knowledge: An Essay on Religious Epistemology.* Leiden, Neth.: E. J. Brill, 1995.
Blocker, Jane. *Seeing Witness: Visuality and the Ethics of Testimony.* Minneapolis: University of Minnesota Press, 2009.
Bockmuehl, Markus. *Seeing the Word: Refocusing New Testament Study.* Grand Rapids, MI: Baker Academic, 2006.
Browning, Elizabeth Barrett. "From Aurora Leigh." In *The Oxford Book of English Mystical Verse.* Edited by D. H. S. Nicholson and A. H. E. Lee, 150–52. Oxford: The Clarendon Press, 1917.
Brueggemann, Walter. *Texts under Negotiation: The Bible and Postmodern Imagination.* Minneapolis: Fortress Press, 1993.
Buechner, Frederick. *The Eyes of the Heart: A Memoir of the Lost and Found.* New York: HarperOne, 2000.
———. *The Face of Jesus: A Life Story.* Brewster, MA: Paraclete Press, 2005.
Camilleri, Charlo. "To Be is to Gaze and Be Gazed at: Vision in Maria Maddelana de' Pazzi's Mysticism." *Studies in Spirituality,* 19, 35–46, 2009.
Casey, Michael. *Fully Human Fully Divine: An Interactive Christology.* Mulgrave, Aus.: John Garrett Publishing, 2004.
Caviness, Madeline. "Artist: To See, Hear, and Know All at Once." In *Voice of the Living Light: Hildegard of Bingen and Her World.* Edited by Barbara Newman. 110–24. Berkeley: University of California Press, 1998.
Clark, Francis. *Godfaring: On Reason, Faith and Sacred Being.* London: St. Pauls Publishing, 2000.
Claudel, Paul. In D. C. Schindler, "Truth and the Christian Imagination: The Reformation of Causality and the Iconoclasm of the Spirit." *Communio: International Catholic Review,* Winter, no. 33 (2006), 521–39.
Clement, Olivier. *The Roots of Christian Mysticism: Texts from the Patristic Era with Commentary.* New York: New City Press, 1993.
Coolman, Boyd Taylor. *Knowing God by Experience: the Spiritual Senses in the Theology of William of Auxerre.* The Catholic University of America Press, Washington DC, 2004.
Dawkins, Richard. *The God Delusion.* London: Bantam Press, 2006.

Detzler, Wayne. "Enlightenment." In *Dictionary of the Christian Church*. Edited by J. D. Douglas, 343–44. Exeter, UK: The Paternoster Press, 1974.

Devenish, Stuart C. "The Contribution of Spirituality to Our Understanding of Human Flourishing: the Perspective of Christian Theology." In *Beyond Well-being: Spirituality's Contribution to Human Flourishing*. Edited by Maureen Miner et al., Charlotte, NC: Information Age Publishing, 2012 [forthcoming].

Dillard, Annie. *Pilgrim at Tinker Creek*. London: Picador/Pan Books, 1975.

———. *Teaching a Stone to Talk*. London: Picador/Pan Books, 1982.

Dixon, W. MacNeile. *The Human Situation: Problems of Life and Destiny*. Sydney: Angus & Robertson, 1938.

Dyrness, William A. *Poetic Theology: God and the Poetics of Everyday Life*. Grand Rapids, MI: Wm. B. Eerdmans, 2001.

Eckhart, Meister. *Selected Writings*. London: Penguin Books, 1994.

Emonet, Pierre-Marie. *God Seen in the Mirror of the World: An Introduction to the Philosophy of God*. New York: Herder and Herder, 1997.

Ferrer, Jorge N. "Spiritual Knowing as Participatory Enaction." In *The Participatory Turn: Spirituality, Mysticism, Religious Studies*. Edited by Jorge N. Ferrer and Jacob H. Sherman. 135–69. New York: State University of New York, 2008.

Ferrer, Jorge N., and Jacob H. Sherman, eds. *The Participatory Turn: Spirituality, Mysticism, Religious Studies*. New York: State University of New York, 2008.

Fisher, Myra. "Who Are the Letter Writers?" Reported by David Astle. *Sunday Life Sun-Herald Magazine*, May 15, 2005, 25.

Fodor, Jim. "Reading the Scriptures: Rehearsing Identity, Practising Character." In *The Blackwell Companion to Christian Ethics*. Edited by Stanley Hauerwas and Samuel Wells, 155–69. Oxford: Blackwell, 2004.

Ford-Grabowsky, Mary. *Stations of the Light: Renewing the Ancient Christian Practice of the Via Lucis as a Spiritual Tool for Today*. New York: NYC Doubleday, 2005.

Gabriel, Yiannis, and Lang, Tim. *The Unmanageable Consumer*. London: Sage, 2006.

Hall, Gary P. "Choosing Life or Second Life? Discipleship and Agency in a Mediated Culture." *International Review of Mission*, Jan–Apr 2008, 97, 7–20.

Hauerwas, Stanley, and William Willimon. *Resident Aliens: A Provocative Christian Assessment of Culture and Ministry for People Who Know that Something is Wrong*. Nashville: Abingdon Press, 1991.

Hays, Richard B. *The Moral Vision of the New Testament: A Contemporary Introduction to New Testament Ethics*. New York: Continuum Books, 1997.

Hobbes, Thomas. *Leviathan: or the Matter, Forme and Power of a Common-Wealth Ecclesiasticall and Civill*. London: Andrew Crooke, 1651.

Hopkins, Gerard Manley. "God's Grandeur." In *The Poems of Gerard Manley Hopkins*. Fourth edition. Edited by W. H. Gardner and N. H. MacKenzie, 66. London: Oxford University Press, 1970.

Kelcourse, Felicity, B. "Finding Faith: Life-Cycle Stages in Body, Mind and Soul." In *Human Development and Faith: Life-Cycle Stages in Body, Mind, and Soul*. Edited by Felicity B. Kelcourse. 59–90. St. Louis, MO: Chalice Press, 2004.

Kerkhofs, Jan. *A Horizon of Kindly Light: A Spirituality for Those with Questions*. London: SCM Press, 1999.

Kettle, David J. *Western Culture in Gospel Context: Towards the Conversion of the West*. Eugene, OR: Cascade Books, 2011.

Kreider, Alan. *Worship and Evangelism in Pre-Christendom*. Alcuin/GROW Liturgical Studies Series. Cambridge, UK: Grove Books, 1995.

Lansdown, Andrew. "Fantasy and its Place in the Christian Imagination." Conference paper, *Lewis for Educators*, Sydney, July 2006. No pages. Online: http://www.cslewistoday.com/blog/andrew-lansdown-on-fantasy-and-its-place-in-christian-imagination.

Larkin, Ernest, E. "Discernment of Spirits." In *A Dictionary of Christian Spirituality*. Edited by Gordon S. Wakefield, 115–16. London: SCM Press, 1983.

LeGuin, Ursula. In Kathleen R. Fisher, *The Inner Rainbow: The Imagination in Christian Life*, 6. New York: Paulist Press, 1983.

Leonard, Bill J. *Becoming Christian: Dimensions of Spiritual Formation*. Louisville, KY: Westminster/John Knox Press, 1990.

Levy, Sandra, M. *Imagination and the Journey of Faith*. Grand Rapids, MI: Wm. B. Eerdmans, 2008.

Lewis, C. S. *Mere Christianity*. London: Collins/Fontana, 1970.

———. *Surprised by Joy*. London: Geoffrey Bles, 1955.

———. *They Asked for a Paper: Papers and Addresses*. London: Geoffrey Bles, 1962.

———. *The Voyage of the Dawn Treader*. The third book of *The Chronicles of Narnia* (with illustrations hand-colored by the artist Pauline Baynes). London: HarperCollins Children's Books, n.d.

Lindbeck, George, A. *The Nature of Doctrine: Religion and Theology in a Postliberal Age*. Philadelphia: The Westminster Press, 1984.

Lindsley, Art. "The Importance of Imagination for C. S. Lewis and for Us." *Knowing & Doing: A Teaching Quarterly for Discipleship of Heart and Mind*. No pages. Online: http://184.73.229.140/webfm_send/52.

Loder, James F. *The Transforming Moment*. San Francisco: Harper and Row, 1981.

Lonergan, Bernard. "Lonergan Responds." In Foundations of Theology. Papers from the International Lonergan Congress 1970. Edited by Philip McShane, S. J. 223–34. Dublin: Gill and MacMillan.

MacDonald, George. *A Dish of Orts: Papers on the Imagination, and on Shakespeare*. Whitefish, MT: Kessinger, n.d.

McIntyre, John. *Faith, Theology and Imagination*. Edinburgh: Handsel, 1987.

McKane, William. *Proverbs: A New Approach*. London: SCM, 1970.

Meek, Esther Lightcap. *Loving to Know: Covenant Epistemology*. Eugene, OR: Cascade Books, 2011.

Merton, Thomas. *The Seven Storey Mountain*. San Diego: Harcourt Brace, 1976.

Muggeridge, Malcolm. *Conversion: A Spiritual Journey*. London: Collins, 1988.

———. *A Third Testament*. London: Collins and British Broadcasting, 1977.

Newbigin, Lesslie. *The Gospel in a Pluralist Society*. Grand Rapids, MI: Wm. B Eerdmans, 1989.

Newman, John Henry. *Grammar of Ascent*. Garden City, NY: Doubleday, Image Books, 1955.

Nouwen, Henri J. M. *Behold the Beauty of the Lord: Praying with Icons*. Notre Dame, IN: Ave Maria Press, 1987.

Oliver, Mary. "Low Tide." *Amicus Journal*, Winter 1997, Vol. 18, No. 4, 32–43.

Olthius, James. *Knowing Otherwise: Philosophy at the Threshold of Spirituality*. New York: Fordham University Press, 1997.

Otto, Rudolph. *The Idea of the Holy*. London: Oxford University Press, 1923/1980.

Palmer, G. E. H., et al., eds. *The Philokalia*. London: Faber and Faber, 1979.

Pascal, Blaise. *Pensées*. Harmondsworth: Penguin, 1985.
Peace, Richard V. *Conversion in the New Testament*. Grand Rapids, MI: Wm. B. Eerdmans, 1999.
Peterson, Eugene H. *Christ Plays in Ten Thousand Places: A Conversation in Spiritual Theology*. London: Hodder & Stoughton, 2005.
———. *The Message*. Colorado Springs, CO: Christian Art Publishers, 1996.
Phillips, J. B. *New Testament Christianity*. London: Hodder & Stoughton, 1956.
Pike, Kenneth L. "On the Emics and Etics of Pike and Harris." In *Emics and Etics: The Insider/Outsider Debate*. Frontiers of Anthropology 7. Edited by Thomas N. Headland et al., 28–47. Newbury Park, CA: Sage, 1990.
Reno, R. R. "Supernatural Existential," In *The Ordinary Transformed: Karl Rahner and the Christian Vision of Transcendence*. Grand Rapids, MI: Wm. B. Eerdmans, 1995.
Ricoeur, Paul. *The Symbolism of Evil*. Translated by Emerson Buchanan. New York: Harper and Rowe, 1967.
Rush, Ormond. *The Eyes of Faith: the Sense of the Faithful and the Church's Reception of Revelation*. Washington, DC: The Catholic University of America Press, 2009.
Shaw, Luci. "Living in the Gap: Exploring the Space between Earth and Heaven." In *Things in Heaven and Earth: Exploring the Supernatural*. Edited by Harold Fickett, 171–84. Brewster, MA: Paraclete, 1998.
Shoemaker, Samuel, "I Stand at the Door." In *How to Reach Secular People*. George Hunter III. 53–54. Nashville: Abingdon, 1992.
St. Bernard of Clairvaux. *Cantica*, Sermon 74. In Henri de Lubac. *The Discovery of God*. Grand Rapids, MI: Wm. B. Eerdmans, 1956/1996.
St. John Damascene. In Vladimir Lossky, *The Vision of God*. Leighton Buzzard, Bedfordshire, UK: The Faith Press; American Orthodox Book Service, 1973.
Sustainable Change. Christian Blind Mission (CBM). Winter 2011.
Taylor, Charles. *A Secular Age*. Cambridge, MA: Belknap, 2007.
Thomson, Francis, "In No Strange Land," In *The Lion Book of Christian Poetry*. Edited by Mary Batchelor. Oxford: Lion, 2005.
Tolkien, J. R. R. *The Lord of the Rings*. London: HarperCollins, 1991.
von Balthasar, Hans Urs. *Theo-Drama : Theological Dramatic Theory: The dramatis personae: Man in God*. Vol 1. San Francisco: Ignatius, 1990.
von Rad, Gerhard. *Wisdom in Israel*. Nashville: Abingdon, 1972.
Walling, Terry. Leader Breakthru, No pages. Online: http://www.leaderbreakthru.com/. From a real-time seminar on leadership transitions in Sydney, September 2011.
Walsh, Brian J. and Richard Middleton. *The Transforming Vision*. Downers Grove, IL: Intervarsity, 1984.
Watts, John D. W., *Isaiah 1–33*. Word Biblical Commentary. Waco, TX: Word Books, 1985.
Weil, Simone. *Waiting for God*. Translated by Emma Craufurd. New York: HarperCollins, 2001.
Whitehead, Alfred North. *Science and the modern world*. New York: Free Press, 1967.
Wilkins, Robert L. *The Christians as the Romans Saw Them*. New Haven, CT, and London: Yale University Press, 1984.
Willard, Dallas. *Renovation of the Heart*. Leicester, UK: IVP, 2002.
Willimon, William H., *Shaped by the Bible*. Nashville: Abingdon 1990.
Wisdom of Solomon, The Apocrypha. (Revised Version). London: Oxford University Press, 1964.

www.ingramcontent.com/pod-product-compliance
Lightning Source LLC
Chambersburg PA
CBHW070943160426
43193CB00011B/1791